Singing Down the Barriers

Singing Down the Barriers

A Guide to Centering African American Song for Concert Performers

Emery Stephens and Caroline Helton

ROWMAN & LITTLEFIELD
Lanham • Boulder • New York • London

Published by Rowman & Littlefield
An imprint of The Rowman & Littlefield Publishing Group, Inc.
4501 Forbes Boulevard, Suite 200, Lanham, Maryland 20706
www.rowman.com

86-90 Paul Street, London EC2A 4NE

Copyright © 2023 by The Rowman & Littlefield Publishing Group, Inc.

All rights reserved. No part of this book may be reproduced in any form or by any electronic or mechanical means, including information storage and retrieval systems, without written permission from the publisher, except by a reviewer who may quote passages in a review.

British Library Cataloguing in Publication Information Available

Library of Congress Cataloging-in-Publication Data
Names: Stephens, Emery, author. | Helton, Caroline, author.
Title: Singing down the barriers : a guide to centering African American song for concert performers / Emery Stephens and Caroline Helton.
Description: Lanham : Rowman & Littlefield Publishers, 2023. | Includes bibliographical references and index.
Identifiers: LCCN 2023005087 (print) | LCCN 2023005088 (ebook) | ISBN 9781538169919 (cloth) | ISBN 9781538169926 (paperback) | ISBN 9781538169933 (ebook)
Subjects: LCSH: African Americans—Music—History and criticism. | Vocal music—United States—History and criticism. | African Americans—Music—Appreciation.
Classification: LCC ML3556 .S866 2023 (print) | LCC ML3556 (ebook) | DDC 782.42089/96073—dc23/eng/20230201
LC record available at https://lccn.loc.gov/2023005087
LC ebook record available at https://lccn.loc.gov/2023005088

Dedicated to the memory of our mothers: to Margaret Stephens, who encouraged Emery to pursue music education, and to Nancy Helton, who taught her children to set an example.

Contents

	List of Figures	xiii
	Acknowledgments	xv
	Preface	xvii
Introduction	What Is the "Singing Down the Barriers" Project?	xxi
	Obstacles of Ignorance	xxiii
	Obstacles of Ambivalence	xxv
	Singing Down the Barriers 1.0	xxvi

SECTION I   HISTORICAL FOUNDATIONS AND CONTEXT

Chapter 1	American Music in the Nineteenth Century through an Inclusive Lens	3
	Antebellum Black Americans and Their Musical World	5
	Antebellum White Americans and the Origins of Blackface Minstrelsy	8
	Emancipation and Reconstruction	10
Chapter 2	The Early Twentieth Century: Race, Music, Popular Culture, and the Harlem Renaissance	15
	A Curated Early Twentieth-Century Timeline	15
	The Promise of a New Century: The Pursuit of Education, Respect, and Economic Autonomy	17

viii ～ Contents

	Interracial Collaborations and the Birth of a Music Economy Based on Black Music	19
	Reality Sets In: Barriers from Stereotypes, Segregation, and Jim Crow	22
	The New Negro and Vocal Concert Music	24
Chapter 3	Post-War, the Civil Rights Era, and Beyond	35
	Black Music and Its Impact in the Post–World War II Era	35
	Jazz: Swing to Bebop	35
	Popular Music: Rhythm and Blues to Rock and Roll	37
	Concert Music: Barriers of Racism, Classicism, and Politics	38
	The Civil Rights Era and the Power of Black Song	40
	Civil Rights and the Concert Hall	42
	The 1970s and Beyond: Black Song in a "Colorblind" Culture	44
	The Twenty-First Century: Walk the Walk, Sing the Songs	49

SECTION II INSTITUTIONAL INTERVENTIONS

Chapter 4	The Academy as an Agent of Restorative Justice through Pedagogy, Performance, Research, and Community Engagement	55
	Pedagogy	55
	Performance	58
	Informed Research	59
	Community Engagement	62
Chapter 5	Influence and Inspiration: Understanding Context and Cultural Influences in Classical American Vocal Music	67
	Teaching What We Know: How the Academy Assigns Value and Replicates Established Hierarchies	67
	Culture and the Canon	68
	Entry Points for Centering Black Composers of Classic Song and Opera: Acknowledging the Academy as a Historically White Space	71
	Song Case Studies	73

	Getting to Know You: Amy Beach and Florence Price	73
	Influence and Inspiration:	
	The Beauty of Shared Culture	74
	The Special Case of Black Opera in Academic Concert Settings	75
	Rich Man, Poor Man	76
	A Tale of Two Bobs	77
Chapter 6	Centering the African American Experience: Spirituals and Non-Classical Genres in the Voice Studio	81
	Spirituals as Common Ground: Creating a Pathway to Learning History through a Black Lens	81
	Entering the Black Space of the Concert Spiritual with Cultural Humility and Knowledge	82
	Black Theology	83
	Notes on Performance Practice	84
	Concert Spiritual Settings: Case Studies across Time and Styles	86
	Two Arrangements of "Ride On, King Jesus": H.T. Burleigh and Hall Johnson	87
	Two Arrangements of "Deep River": J. Rosamond Johnson and Moses Hogan	93
	Spirituals as a Path to Non-Classical Genres in the Voice Studio	98
	Musical Theatre Meets Black Popular Song Genres	100
	Case Studies in Popular Song: Learning Contemporary Musical Theatre Vocalism, Style, and Musicianship from the Greats of Jazz, R&B, Soul, and Gospel	101

SECTION III STRATEGIES FOR CREATING COMMUNITY AND BUILDING MUSIC ECOSYSTEMS

Chapter 7	Allyship, Permission, and Informed Performance Practice	107
	Allyship	108
	Case Studies: Engaging Experts in the Field	111
	Randye Jones	111
	Reinaldo Moya	112
	Glendower Jones	113

	Lifelong Education and the Role of Cultural Humility	114
	Permission and Shared Responsibility	115
	Informed Performance Practice	116
Chapter 8	**Facilitating Meaningful Conversations and Building Relationships: How to Create Vibrant Music Ecosystems in the Academy**	123
	Community Building for Administration and Faculty: Walking the Walk	125
	Developing Deep Listening Skills	125
	Entering Group Discussions	127
	Living Allyship through Action: Activities for Faculty and Administrators	128
	Approaches to Student Learning: Classroom Teaching, Student Research, and Performance Projects	129
	Learning Outcomes	129
	Classroom Activities	129
	Research Projects	132
	Artistry with an American Accent: Creative Programming Ideas	133
Chapter 9	**Community Music Engagement, Data Collection, and Audience Development**	138
	Community Arts Education	136
	Research and Performance Preparation	140
	Discussing Race-Specific Performance Projects	143
	Setting the Table: Guest Speakers, Teaching Artists, and Cultural Bearers	144
	Creating Audiences and Equal Opportunities	145
	Relationship Building toward Networking	146
	Attending Concerts in the Community	149
	Final Thoughts	149
	Selected Bibliography and Resources	151
	Selected Song Anthologies and Collections	157

Glossary	159
Index	163
About the Authors	173

Figures

Figure 1.1.	African American Music Timeline (Maultsby and Burnim)	4
Figure 2.1.	"Mother to Son" (excerpt A)	27
Figure 2.2.	"Mother to Son" (excerpt B)	28
Figure 2.3.	"Mother to Son" (excerpt C)	29
Figure 2.4.	"Mother to Son" (excerpt D)	30
Figure 2.5.	"Mother to Son" (excerpt E)	31
Figure 3.1.	1993 Met Competition Photo	46
Figure 3.2.	Ray M. Wade, Jr.	47
Figure 4.1.	Pedagogical Framework	57
Figure 5.1.	Representative African American Composers and White Composers	72
Figure 6.1.	Marian Anderson	88
Figure 6.2.	Harry T. Burleigh	89
Figure 6.3.	Hall Johnson	90
Figure 6.4.	James Weldon Johnson	94
Figure 6.5.	J. Rosamond Johnson	95

Figure 6.6.	Moses Hogan	97
Figure 7.1.	Education, Dialogue, and Performance	109
Figure 7.2.	"Early in the Mornin'" (Excerpts A and B)	118
Figure 7.3.	"Early in the Mornin'" (Excerpts C and D)	119
Figure 8.1.	Institutional Music Ecosystem (in the "Academy")	124
Figure 9.1.	Community-Based Music Ecosystem	141

Acknowledgments

From Emery Stephens:

    I express my profound gratitude to Caroline Helton, whose longtime friendship has fostered collaboration on music and race discussions with students and teaching colleagues and the study and informed performance of vocal concert music by Black composers. Our work is respectful, inspiring, and intentional. Many people have impacted my lived experience, but I would like to mention a few. I owe a debt of gratitude to my music teachers, who saw a spark in me and believed in my naive abilities, and the spiritual communities who poured the divine gift of music into me. Thank you to my doctoral advisor, George Shirley, at the University of Michigan, who encouraged me to pursue performance research to become the principal investigator of my first African American Art Song survey. To my influential voice teacher, Daniel Washington, whose vocal insight and performance record supported my research and realized my impact as a Black singer and teacher in classical music. And indeed, I stand on the shoulders of those culture bearers who have led me to African American classical repertoire, including Willis Patterson, Robert Honeysucker, Ruth Hamilton, Vivian Taylor, George Shirley, and leading performance scholars Louise Toppin, Darryl Taylor, Donny Ray Albert, and many more. I am most appreciative of the St. Olaf College community, including my colleagues who provided support through a professional development grant and a course release to complete this incredible writing opportunity. I honor past and present students, including those researchers from various institutions who demonstrated an interest in American song through the

Black lens. And finally, a special thank you to my partner, Chuck Snelling, who encourages me to fulfill my passion and live my best life.

From Caroline Helton:

My acknowledgments must begin by thanking my dear friend and colleague, Emery Stephens, whose passion for and knowledge of this repertoire is matched by his generosity of spirit. He is a teacher to his core, and it has been an honor to walk alongside him in this work for the past twenty years. But our partnership might never have flourished had I not been encouraged by two of the greatest living African American luminaries of classical singing who were my mentors during my doctoral studies at the University of Michigan: George Shirley and Willis Patterson. They not only gave me permission as a White singer to perform this repertoire, but they charged me with the mission of passing it on to my students. The environment at the University of Michigan is a very special one in which I have had the great good fortune to work beside not only George Shirley, but the late Shirley Verrett, and Louise Toppin, who is one of this generation's leading experts in this repertoire and a truly tireless, brilliant advocate. That "Michigan Difference" also includes my wonderful current and former students, who have been incredibly supportive and involved in this work over the years and from whom I have learned so much. Another group to whom I owe the deepest gratitude are my *Singing Justice* colleagues, Naomi André, Stephen Berrey, Tyrese Byrd, Mark Clague, Christie Finn, Thomas Hampson, Cody Jones, Traci Lombré, and Samantha Williams (along with Louise Toppin). The knowledge I have gained throughout our work together was indispensable to the completion of this book, and without their support and collaboration I could have never achieved this milestone. And lastly, my husband, Matt Kaplan, who was the first to recognize the significance of Emery's and my work, and who gave us the evocative title for our project. He has been my constant sounding board, editor, and cheerleader.

We sincerely thank Michael Tan, Associate Acquisitions Editor, and Rowman & Littlefield for supporting and managing our project.

Preface

I, too, sing America.

I am the darker brother.
They send me to eat in the kitchen
When company comes,
But I laugh,
And eat well,
And grow strong.

Tomorrow,
I'll be at the table
When company comes.
Nobody'll dare
Say to me,
"Eat in the kitchen,"
Then.

Besides,
They'll see how beautiful I am
And be ashamed—

I, too, am America.

–Langston Hughes

As we write in the summer of 2022, American society is consumed with yet another racial reckoning, long overdue, much needed, and, of course, highly controversial. In the wake of nationwide protests over the murder of George Floyd at the hands of the police, the advent of the Black Lives Matter movement, and all the introspection these events have set into motion, every aspect of American society is either doing the difficult work of coming to terms with systemic racism or doing its best to fight that process. As two singers and voice teachers—one Black and one White—who have spent many years performing and teaching about the rich body of song produced by African American composers and leading discussions about the multifaceted barriers and benefits to studying and performing this repertoire, we are both encouraged and dismayed by the moment in which we find ourselves. One great cause for encouragement in this cultural moment is the astounding increase in research, publication, performance, and general awareness of the contributions of African American composers. But in order for all this knowledge to infuse and transform our perceptions of the canon of song literature, we in the arts must also do the work of examining how racism has shaped our culture not just in terms of Jim Crow–type exclusion of Black composers, but how the legacy of the inhumane and immoral practice of chattel slavery in the United States gave rise to pervasive cultural perceptions and stereotypes around performance. We feel like the concert stage is the most accessible venue to work out these cultural conflicts, because when one sings in concert, no matter the genre, the purpose of that performance is to tell a story, and storytellers do not have to resemble the characters they embody in order to transport you into the world of the story.

The story we're telling in this book, that of African American song, begins with the spiritual, which inevitably recalls slavery to the front of our minds and brings an ugly truth into the space of the concert hall. Discomfort with confronting that legacy as well as the reverberations of Blackface minstrelsy in the origins of American musical theatre and throughout popular culture have created an ambivalence around performing songs that center the African American experience among Black and White performers alike. In addition to this ambivalence, we must also take into consideration the ignorance of African American contributions to classic song that has resulted from the suppression and erasure of Black composers from the classical music canon because of segregation in the concert halls and exclusion from the publishing houses. It will take a conscious and sustained effort to fully explore the causes of this ignorance and ambivalence and find solutions to achieve lasting culture change; our book strives to provide a model for what that work could look like.

The work begins with understanding the historical foundations, context, and contributing factors to our society's dysfunctional culture at the nexus of race and vocal performance, which is the subject of the first section of our book. In the introduction, we describe the origins of the "Singing Down the Barriers" project, and follow with three chapters that examine the history of American song through a lens that centers the musical contributions of African Americans and reveals how fundamentally influential those contributions have been. Chapter 1 considers the opposing ethoses of two bodies of song that proliferated in the nineteenth century and were the first to represent an American musical identity to the rest of the world: African American spirituals and minstrel songs. The second chapter unpacks the turn of the century and the Harlem Renaissance, focusing on the segregated reality that Black composers, performers, and songwriters inhabited and how they asserted their dignity and creativity in the realm of concert music while also navigating the racialized commercial market of American musical theater and Tin Pan Alley; however, the chapter also highlights the prevalence and importance of interracial musical collaborations during that period. Chapter 3 covers a longer span of time that begins with the post-war period of African American disillusionment and White backlash leading to the civil rights movement and goes on to examine the continued lack of Black representation in the musical canon of the predominantly White conservatories as well as the position of African American performers and composers in America's "colorblind" society from the 1980s to Barack Obama's presidency.

In the second section, we present approaches to centering African American song with the goal of promoting restorative justice in the academy. Chapter 4 defines the central role that predominantly White institutions play in pedagogy, performance, and research, and how they can use that power for positive change. Chapter 5 considers the culture of those predominantly White institutions and offers practical suggestions for reframing the traditional recital programming model to include the classical contributions of African American composers. In the sixth chapter, we look specifically at concert settings of spirituals and how they form a link from classical genres to non-classical genres in the voice studio, and suggest ways of connecting the artistry of African American icons of Black popular music to the study of contemporary musical theater vocalism and style.

The chapters in the third section, "Strategies for Creating Community and Building Music Ecosystems," seek to clearly define crucial issues to consider when amplifying the music of African Americans and provide models for creating trust and establishing interracial partnerships in your communities. Chapter 7 examines the concepts of allyship, permission, and informed performance practice, and chapter 8 breaks down the process of building a music ecosystem within the academy so that all stakeholders—from the administration to the faculty to the students they teach—can play a role in bringing positive change to the academy's culture. The final chapter considers how communities outside the academy can expand the reach of African American song, leveraging local grant funding, expanding networks, and building audiences for innovative and relevant programming of music by Black creators.

Our work with the "Singing Down the Barriers" project is completely collaborative, and necessarily so, because our example of interracial partnership is vital to its success going forward. With writing this book, our collaborative work took the form of individual writing tasks—Caroline authored the front matter and chapters 1, 2, 3, and 5, and Emery authored chapters 4, 8, and 9, and was the lead author on the two chapters that we wrote together, chapters 6 and 7—coupled with constant communication about resources and feedback on the other's work. Although there is a lot of information in our book, it is not an encyclopedia; our goal is rather to help the reader contextualize vocal concert repertoire (as well as non-classical genres) by African American composers, and take action to make lasting and meaningful changes not only to the canon of American song, but to the culture of its performance. It is not enough to simply learn the songs; singers of all ethnicities must understand our shared history, grapple with its legacy, study texts and music, empathize with the creators, and find the courage to listen to and support each other much more intentionally, with the common goal of "singing America" in all its diversity.

Introduction

What Is the "Singing Down the Barriers" Project?

Our work began back in 2004 in a seminar that Caroline was teaching that comprised students in Emery's Doctor of Musical Arts cohort at the University of Michigan School of Music, Theatre & Dance. The subject of Emery's final presentation was the origin and performance practice of concert spirituals,[1] and he concluded it with an enthusiastic invitation to his colleagues to perform this highly expressive American repertoire. Emery was the only Black student in the class, and the rest of the students responded to his invitation by saying, "We can't perform spirituals because we're not Black." Emery was struck by their hesitancy, especially immediately following a lecture that provided historical context as well as addressing style and diction considerations appropriate to the repertoire, as classical singers are trained in all other genres of song. Perhaps because it was a small class of people who knew each other very well, Emery decided to engage with this hesitancy by asking a powerfully fundamental question: "Why not?" It is this question that has driven our work from that point forward.

Emery set about trying to answer that question by creating and distributing a survey to a diverse network of classical singers and voice teachers. The questions on the survey sought to probe the emotional reactions of singers from all racial backgrounds to crossing the color barrier in performance; the purpose of the survey was to discover what inhibited singers from performing this repertoire, the benefits being, at least on the surface, self-evident:

1. Spirituals represent the largest body of American folk song,[2] so the songs are culturally relatable.
2. The songs are in English, so they are accessible to undergraduate voice students who haven't begun their training in the lyric diction of Italian, German, and French.
3. Spirituals are musically accessible to singers and audiences alike because of the simplicity and beauty of the melodies.
4. From a pedagogical standpoint, singing concert spirituals builds good vocal technique because they were written for trained solo singers to perform in concert, and demand a high level of expressive control in range, dynamics, articulation, and emotional communication.
5. Because spirituals have been set by classical African American composers for concert performance since the turn of the twentieth century, there is a great variety of settings to choose from to benefit a singer at any point in their[3] development, ranging from majestically simple in rhythm and harmony (such as "Deep River" by H.T. Burleigh) to extremely complex musically and challenging vocally (such as "Peter go ring-a dem bells" from *Cantata* by John Carter).
6. Concert performance is the ideal setting for exploring identities that do not match that of the performer. In art song, the performer sings from the perspective of whichever characters are represented in the poem, sometimes many different ones, in the manner of a storyteller (such as the beloved Schubert songs "Erlkönig"[4] and "Der Tod und das Mädchen"[5]) rather than an actor who portrays one role in a play.

It was at this point that Emery asked Caroline to be his partner in examining the data and devising an approach that could lead to widespread performance of the repertoire. It seemed very natural that we should be undertaking this work together at the University of Michigan, an institution that has been at the forefront of championing the song literature of African American composers since the 1970s, when Voice professor and Associate Dean Willis Patterson[6] was one of the first faculty in the country to offer a vocal literature course in the song repertoire of African American composers at a predominantly White institution. Caroline received a Doctor of Musical Arts degree in Vocal Performance from the University of Michigan in 1998, and Dean Patterson was on her dissertation committee. But interestingly, in a way that would shed light on their future research, Caroline (who is White) had never availed herself of Dean Patterson's class or used his resources to explore the repertoire of African American composers, so she was by no means an effective advocate for this literature when Emery was in her seminar. Her story is no doubt common among students and educators at predominantly White institutions at that time; she was the archetype of the well-meaning liberal college professor who, being well informed about the struggles of African Americans to overcome systemic racism, strongly supported civil rights and equality for Americans of all backgrounds. Yet she was passive when it came to performing the repertoire herself, and it took Emery's invitation to join him in his research for her to begin to understand the forces at work that were keeping African American song literature obscure and the canon of American song segregated.

As we analyzed the data from Emery's survey, some clear trends emerged that gave us trails to follow. The respondents represented a diverse sample of the population of classical singers and voice teachers, so we were able to discern trends of responses within demographic groups. What surprised us is that Black and White singers alike described various barriers to performing the repertoire, and those barriers broke down into two basic categories: ignorance and ambivalence.

Obstacles of Ignorance

Normally, ignorance is considered a pretty simple problem to fix. You can check out a book and study the repertoire and your job is done. But even this first step of finding basic resources (until very recently) could lead to a dead end when it comes to finding repertoire by African American composers. If you have ever studied classical singing, we invite you to ask yourself this question: were you assigned songs by Black American composers, or were they on your syllabi in your music history or literature classes? If you attended a predominantly White institution and if you belong to the generation of most faculty today, the answer is, in all likelihood, no. American song anthologies and syllabi are filled with a wide variety of songs by White male composers that are revered as the canon of American song, but that is by no means an accurate representation of the gamut of American song composition. From the late nineteenth century, African American composers were actively writing songs and spiritual settings, as well as operas, symphonies, and chamber music, but, except for the spiritual settings, these pieces were neither widely performed nor published. Exclusion of the repertoire by White publishing houses effectively expunged African American composers from the written record of music that forms the basis of the canon taught in our colleges and universities, which led to an erasure of the repertoire from the diverse panorama of American song.

Besides the ignorance borne of erasure, there is an ignorance borne of segregation both physically, in concert halls before the civil rights movement, and culturally, in how our attitudes and assumptions have been formed about what constitutes "classical" music. From folk song to popular song to the concert hall, there is ample evidence for the interconnectedness of Black and White musicians, composers, and performers. America's largest body of folk song, the spiritual, is the creative patrimony of enslaved Africans, yet these songs are universally beloved for their melodic beauty and emotional power. From Tin Pan Alley to Hip Hop, collaborations, inspirations, and, yes, appropriations from Black styles and creators are the hallmark of American popular music. Classical repertoire is similarly dependent on Black contributions that infuse and signify the American voice: Dvořák's *New World Symphony* would not have been possible without his collaboration with H.T. Burleigh, who exposed Dvořák to spirituals[7]; in the early twentieth century, jazz took the old world by storm and captured the imagination of such revered composers as Debussy, Ravel, Milhaud, and even Shostakovich; George Gershwin, who learned orchestration from William Grant Still, was steeped in jazz from his collaborations with a number of jazz musicians, most notably his friend James P. Johnson, the legendary pianist and pioneer of stride piano. This is not even to mention the great American opera *Porgy and Bess*, every aspect of which highlights our history of racial dynamics around musical language and performance. With all this musical influence and interconnectedness, one would think Black concert music would be celebrated here in the United States; yet, due to an attitude that equates "Black music" with "popular music" (making it therefore unworthy of the concert hall), operas and symphonic works by African Americans have rarely been programmed by major American symphony orchestras and opera companies, constituting an erasure through lack of exposure. To quote a Guinean proverb, "We cannot love that which we do not know."[8]

For a thought experiment, imagine that we had learned about Black composers in school and heard their works performed in concert halls. We would then have a foundation of aural and intellectual experience to ameliorate the next barrier of ignorance: performance practice and style. To be sure, this is a topic to be addressed carefully and respectfully due to the legacy of Blackface minstrelsy in the United States, and we will offer detailed guidance on this subject in subsequent chapters. There are, as well, recent publications[9] that provide excellent instruction for the performance practice and style of spirituals and art songs by African American composers. However, it is undeniable that many singers don't have any idea where to start, and not just because of racial ambivalence. Many students associate singing spirituals with the vocal and stylistic practices of Black gospel music, and are unaware of the long tradition of concert spiritual settings. And given that a significant proportion of the texts Black composers have set is based in the Black experience, the performer must have the skills to perform the dialect accurately and convincingly when it is called for, such as in the poetry of Paul Laurence Dunbar.

The last barrier of ignorance stems from the blind spots that result from our society's pervasive lens of Whiteness, which tells us that "White culture is the norm," and everything else is "ethnic." Because the majority of our colleges and universities in the United States could be described as predominantly White institutions, higher education either at best can't help or at worst is invested in replicating the lacunae and biases of American society. Coming to this realization is a process fraught with emotion, one which Robin DiAngelo discusses thoughtfully in her book, *White Fragility*. The assumption is that "if I didn't learn about it from my professors, whom I revere, then repertoire by African American composers must not be as good as the canon I was given," setting up a defensive reaction to those who suggest expanding the canon. Faculty can feel like the foundations of their expertise are being questioned, and that they must replace beloved (i.e., valuable) repertoire with unfamiliar (i.e., less valuable) compositions. When ignorance is baked into the institution's identity, it can be a formidable barrier, like an electric fence rather than a normal fence that one can just climb over.

Obstacles of Ambivalence

Whereas ignorance can be addressed from an intellectual starting point, ambivalence must be understood and confronted from the starting point of emotions, which is obviously much trickier, especially given that the results of Emery's survey showed that the problems of ambivalence clearly did not reside with just one demographic group. In terms of ambivalence, we found that African American classical singers do have a sense of ownership of the repertoire, but reject being pigeonholed or limited to performing it. This is an understandable reaction when one takes into consideration the legacy of Blackface minstrelsy in the United States and the relative lack of artistic control that African American performers have historically been allowed to exert over the material they chose to program. So even before an African American singer takes the first step, they have to navigate a painful emotional dissonance linked to our country's history of racism. Yet even as those historical legacies affect a modern Black singer, that singer is aware that they are very far removed from the conditions of their ancestors, and in some cases may have little to no connection to or experience with spirituals, for example. As we all know, it is frightfully easy to make assumptions about a person's experience based on their skin color, and this happens in the voice studio and the performance world just like it does in society. Imagine being the only Black student in your studio and you're the only one who is assigned a concert spiritual by your teacher, who also doesn't give you any guidance in the performance practice or history of the repertoire because the teacher assumes you already know all about it. That puts you in a very awkward situation on a lot of levels.

White singers experience ambivalence for more obvious reasons, but there is a painful emotional undercurrent to navigate here as well. It is understandable that White singers hesitate to perform spirituals or art songs that portray African American voices in poetry because they recognize and honor the cultural patrimony of African Americans on the one hand, while being keenly aware on the other hand of the danger of putting a foot wrong in today's climate of immediate censure for infractions of cultural appropriation. A trickier and more subconscious emotional reaction stems from the historical practice of Blackface minstrelsy, which is so deeply rooted in our performance culture as well as our society (remember Virginia's governor, Ralph Northam?), but that few people really know that much about. White singers just know it's "wrong" to get up on stage and portray a Black character, and even more so if that character speaks in dialect. Taken together, these barriers of ambivalence exert pressure from both ends of the racial spectrum of performers and create a vicious circle in which no one performs the music, effectively completing the job of erasure that systemic racism started.

Singing Down the Barriers 1.0

After we had digested Emery's data, our first step was to implement a model of education and performance on a small scale, recruiting a diverse group of students from the voice program at the University of Michigan in the fall semester of 2006. We began with group discussions about the history of art songs and spiritual settings by African American composers, also probing their concerns and expectations about the project, and assigning repertoire that they would study over the course of a semester. After their end-of-term performances, we met as a group to debrief their experiences. Their reactions were so encouraging[10] that we decided to present our work to the academic world in various ways. We wrote an article about the project, which was published in a volume on the *Scholarship of Multicultural Teaching and Learning* in 2007,[11] and we gave presentations on our work at the Conference for the International Society of the Scholarship of Teaching and Learning, as well as the African American Art Song Alliance in 2007. Our next step was to try to reach a wider audience by creating a short residency program that we could take to other colleges and universities, thereby planting seeds that we hoped would flourish into gardens of greater musical diversity in Voice programs all over the country.

In terms of addressing the barriers of ignorance and ambivalence, our program was comprehensive. When we were invited to do a residency, we began by providing the Voice faculty with anthologies of songs by African American composers to help them choose repertoire for their students to study as well as a bibliography of reference materials to use in their research that would help them prepare their students for a master class performance dedicated to the repertoire. We also enlisted a Voice teacher and a pianist from the faculty to perform with us on a lecture-recital about the history of African American contributions to song that served as the opening event for our campus visit, and also gave the faculty an opportunity to lead by example. The day after our lecture-recital, we conducted a master class in which the students performed and we offered instruction on the performance practice and style of the songs, and then led discussions about the issues they confronted when studying and performing them, whether it was crossing the color barrier or dialect or even understanding the musical language and cultural references. On occasion we also visited other classes, such as Music History and Music Appreciation, or attended the school choir rehearsals, in order to lecture, discuss, and lead activities intended to deepen the students' understanding of and connection to the repertoire. Rather than neatly solving the problem, our experiences at the different institutions we visited led us to some surprising conclusions about the complexity of advocating for the wider performance of this repertoire and the effectiveness of our model to change the attitudes of faculty and culture of institutions.

Our initial residencies took us to four different types of institutions with varying racial demographics and geographic locations, all of which played a role in the reception and vitality of our work in those communities. The most successful experience we had was at a university situated in a city that serves a diverse population, and where there was participation by faculty and students of all races who engaged in open and thoughtful dialogue in the discussions we facilitated. This was what we had in mind when we developed the content of the residency. But when we visited a university in the rural Midwest with a very homogenous White population, we realized that their experience with the music and their ability to engage with the complexities and challenges of performing it was quite superficial because of their lack of interactions with non-White Americans. On the other end of the spectrum of homogeneity, Emery visited a historically Black college/university and met with resistance to our basic premise that people of all races should sing spirituals or cross the color barrier when they perform songs by African American composers that center the Black experience. Lastly, we visited a university in the deep South that had a diverse population but an all-White faculty that, for the most part, seemed very invested denying that any dialogue was really necessary, because they didn't have a "race problem." The fact that the students very clearly self-segregated in the concert hall, that no one was given repertoire that asked them to cross the color barrier in performance, and that the students seemed guarded in our discussions led us to the conclusion that that community was not ready to entertain our premise at all, much less consider it deeply enough to reject it.

Our hypothesis in 2006 was that, if we spent a few days at an institution, we could ameliorate the problems of ignorance with a lecture-recital and address ambivalence with the examples of faculty and student performances combined with facilitated conversation. We hoped, thereby, to enable the communities to continue with the work on their own, but unfortunately, the results of our efforts showed that a one-off approach only worked to a superficial degree and only with receptive groups and institutions. But given our society's most recent racial awakening, we believe the time is ripe to envision a more proactive, systematic, and inclusive strategy leading to long-term culture change in communities and institutions of higher learning, because it is clear to us from our experience as teachers that we all have something to gain by performing this repertoire. Black singers can represent their cultural history from folk song to art music; White singers can actively learn about the African American experience through doing the background work as well as the empathetic act of singing the words and music of their fellow citizens in a public, respectful acknowledgment of the humanity and struggles of African Americans; and the canon would finally reflect the full diversity of its brilliant composers.

This is not to say that the task will be easy; since our society has never come to terms with the foundational, immoral offense of chattel slavery and its legacy of institutionalized racism, we are now at the point where just singing a song is fraught with cultural and political risk. It would be so much easier not to engage, leaving the work (yet again) to another generation, and guaranteeing the continuation of the status quo. But disruption has an upside: let us take advantage of this moment by linking arms and continuing the work that so many Black artists, composers, intellectuals, and poets began over 150 years ago, heeding the words of the monumental American bass-baritone and activist, Paul Robeson: "Whether singing or acting, race and color prejudices are forgotten. Art is one form against which such barriers do not stand."

Notes

1. Negro spirituals arranged for solo voice with piano accompaniment by classical composers, in the style of art song and requiring a classically trained approach to vocalism.

2. "African American Spirituals," Library of Congress, accessed January 9, 2023, https://www.loc.gov/item/ihas.200197495/.

3. We will employ the singular, non-binary use of the pronoun "they" throughout this text.

4. Poem by J.W. von Goethe (1749–1832).

5. Poem by Matthias Claudius (1740–1815).

6. For more information, please visit Dean Patterson's faculty biography, https://smtd.umich.edu/faculty-profiles/willis-patterson/, and the NATS website, https://www.nats.org/Diversity_Spotlight_-_Willis_Patterson.html.

7. Joseph Horowitz, *Dvořák's Prophecy: And the Vexed Fate of Black Classical Music* (New York: W. W. Norton & Company, Inc., 2022), 9–15.

8. Samuel A. Floyd, *The Power of Black Music: Interpreting Its History from Africa to the United States* (New York: Oxford University Press, 1995), 14.

9. See "Selected Bibliography and Resources."

10. Reactions from the interracial group of students in our focus group in their own words: "This music is powerful because the music is still here, still meaningful and not removed from our cultural experience."

"I was glad to have the opportunity to perform this repertoire with permission, because I've only ever seen Black singers perform it and I've always wanted to be able to."

"'Singing outside the box' breaks cultural barriers and makes it much easier to connect to others. Performing makes you learn way more than just reading about it; it makes the experience much stronger."

"I thought that, since I'm African American, my connection would be automatic, but my insight came through real performance."

"It's much easier for a student to connect with a spiritual or art song by African American composers than an Italian song."

11. Caroline Helton and Emery Stephens, "Singing Down the Barriers: Encouraging Singers of all Racial Backgrounds to Perform Music by African American Composers," *Scholarship of Multicultural Teaching and Learning* (Fall 2007): 111, 73–79. New Directions for Teaching and Learning.

SECTION I

HISTORICAL FOUNDATIONS AND CONTEXT

CHAPTER ONE

American Music in the Nineteenth Century through an Inclusive Lens

Since 1619, Black and White people have inhabited North America, living together in communities, albeit within strict hierarchies, before the Pilgrims even landed on Plymouth Rock. These immigrants (for want of a better word) joined a native population with a culture that spans millennia. Therefore, to think logically of the label "American culture" as historically meaning "White" is ludicrous on its face, because a culture is formed by all the human beings in a community, no matter what roles they play in society. However, societal hierarchy does dictate what gets into the written record, even more so because, on the one hand, Native American and African cultures passed their history down through an oral tradition, and on the other, people who were enslaved were by and large prohibited from learning how to read and write. Erasure of these cultures is therefore baked into our educational system, and it takes a special effort to expand our knowledge to include all the influences and relationships that created the American voice in song. It is astounding that we, two highly educated performers and teachers in the twenty-first century, were inculcated with a canon that included practically no contributions by people of color, perpetuating the idea that art music must always stem from European sources rather than utilizing and celebrating our unique and diverse American cultural material.[1] What follows is a brief summary of American musical culture through the nineteenth century from the African American perspective, directly contrasted with the likely more familiar White points of reference, in an attempt to view the past with a wider, more inclusive lens (see figure 1.1).

4 ~ Chapter One

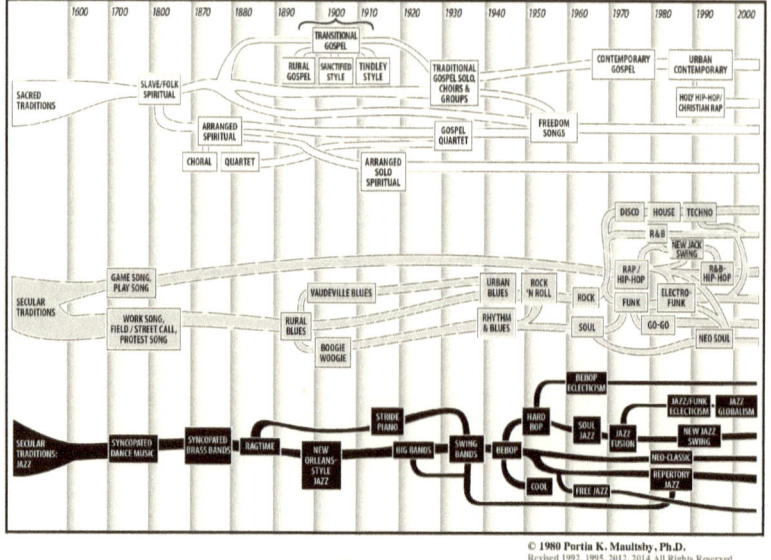

Figure 1.1. African American Music Timeline
Reproduced from AFRICAN AMERICAN MUSIC, 2nd Edition by Mellonee V., Burnim; Portia K., Maultsby, published by Routledge. © Portia K. Maultsby, Ph.D., 1980 (revised 1992, 1995, 2012, 2014), reproduced by arrangement with Taylor & Francis Group.

Music played a central, arguably existential role in African culture. Ethnomusicologist Portia Maultsby's chapter titled "The Translated African Cultural and Musical Past" (in the collection of essays she co-edited with Mellonee Burnim called *African American Music: An Introduction*) begins with a proverb from the Kpelle people of Liberia, West Africa, that claims: "If you build a town and there's no drummer in it, then it's not a town. If you build a town and there's no singer, then it's not a town."[2] Communal music making, especially singing and drumming, was used to form a group's collective identity, to work, to celebrate, to dance, to mourn, to make war, to accompany rituals, and even to heal diseases. When Africans were captured and brought to North America, their enslavers sought to diminish their captives' ability to communicate first linguistically, by separating people from their ethnic groups with their own unique languages, but also musically, by taking away their drums and loud instruments, which the enslavers feared they would use to organize rebellions.[3] Enslaved Africans retained their musical practices, however, adapting them to their cruel circumstances, using them to form new bonds with Africans from other ethnic groups in work and community life. Much as the enslaved Africans had to adapt linguistically, creating a pidgin English dialect to communicate with their captors and other enslaved people, they adapted musically as well, "translating" their African musical practices into new "American" songs for work, worship, and emotional survival.⁴ Even though not all African Americans were enslaved, the vast majority certainly were, so we will begin with a discussion of music among enslaved communities in the nineteenth century.

Antebellum Black Americans and Their Musical World

Of the total U.S. population in 1860 (thirty-one million), enslaved Blacks comprised about 13 percent (four million) and free Blacks comprised about 1.5 percent (five hundred thousand). Within the African American population at that time (4.5 million), enslaved Blacks comprised about 89 percent and free Blacks comprised about 11 percent.⁵ The enslaved population made music rather than consumed it, and that music was primarily vocal. It played various roles in their everyday lives, many of them similar to how song ordered the lives and communities of their African ancestors. For example, work songs kept a consistent beat when group coordination was necessary, while also serving the purpose of maintaining community cohesiveness and morale. While singing work songs was a functional mechanism that could be practiced voluntarily and with a purpose, enslaved people were sometimes required to sing, play instruments, and dance to entertain their enslavers. Their musical talents were prized skills that factored into the monetary value of an enslaved person for their "owners," the evidence for which comes from contemporary newspaper advertisements for their trafficking.

While secular music making could be controlled by the enslavers, religious expression was by and large an avenue for free expression that African Americans poured their heart and soul into over the course of the nineteenth century, producing the body of American folk song referred to as Negro spirituals.⁶ In the late eighteenth and early nineteenth centuries, there was a movement to convert enslaved Africans to Christianity which was successful, to risk understatement. Enslaved Africans clearly identified with the Christian teachings of God's unconditional love ("He's Got the Whole World in His Hands") and Jesus's sacrifice ("He Never Said a Mumblin' Word"), but the Old Testament stories of the travails of the Hebrew slaves were particularly inspiring when it came to coping with their circumstances ("Go Down, Moses"). In fact, some enslavers realized after the fact how problematic the Exodus story could be for their interests and gave worship leaders versions of the Bible with those parts excised.⁷ But the seeds were sown, and the creativity and longing for freedom and dignity of an enslaved population produced a wellspring of song that never seemed to run dry, and that served many functions within their communities besides worship.

Negro spirituals were an expression of community, dignity, and shared humanity. They were catharsis as well as communication, praise as well as sorrow. Amazingly, they were never about retribution. They can be sorted into many categories according to sentiment and subject matter,[8] but one of the most interesting aspects of spirituals is that they often had a double meaning, so that what sounded like innocent religious expression to the slave owner was actually coded information about when and where to meet, when the next opportunity to escape was coming ("Swing Low, Sweet Chariot"), or even how to evade capture ("Wade in de Water"). In any case, enslaved African Americans took comfort from the Christian theology of an afterlife ("City called Heaven"), while also using that theology to affirm their self-worth and envision a better future ("Bye and Bye").

Before Emancipation, there were almost no avenues for African Americans to receive conservatory training. Since enslaved people were not allowed to be educated, the possibility of developing a talent for classical music performance was very rare, although among the handful of classically trained African American antebellum artists there are a couple of fascinating individuals born into slavery whose gifts were widely recognized, such as soprano Elizabeth Taylor Greenfield (1809–1876) and pianist Thomas "Blind Tom" Bethune (1849–1908). Elizabeth Taylor Greenfield was born into slavery but freed as a child, and she received musical training while remaining in the household of her former mistress, E.H. Greenfield. Her singing talent was recognized when she began performing at private parties, after which she undertook a concert tour, promoted with the moniker "The Black Swan," in order to equate her with Jenny Lind,[9] who was known as "The Swedish Nightingale." (Jenny Lind was of course the operatic soprano who became wildly famous when she was brought to the United States in 1850 by P.T. Barnum for a tour that lasted nearly two years.) Through the patronage of the Duchess of Sutherland and Harriet Beecher Stowe, Elizabeth Taylor Greenfield went to study in London, and in 1854 became the first African American to perform for British royalty.[10]

Thomas Bethune was truly a musical savant, who, because he was blind and not fit for work on the plantation, was granted access to a piano when he showed interest as a child, and then became one of the most well-known performing pianists of the nineteenth century and was the first African American to give a command performance at the White House, for President James Buchanan. Bethune's prodigious gifts were treated as anomalies of the sideshow variety, playing on the trope of the "noble savage."[11] In his case as well as others, the promoters profited more than the performers, and the performers also didn't have any authority to dictate their audiences. For example, because of segregation and the pro-slavery leanings of her promoter, African American patrons were not allowed to attend the Black Swan's concerts. This lack of control in terms of exploitative marketing and "Whites Only" audiences is yet another historical and deep-rooted cause for feelings of anger and distrust underlying accusations of cultural appropriation today.

In the case of the free Black population, their circumstances differed from region to region. In the free states, Black Americans had autonomy to form civic and religious groups as well as organize politically and tended to live in segregated neighborhoods in urban areas. Because they were competing with White immigrants for jobs that required skilled labor, they tended to be poorer than their free Black counterparts in the slave states.[12] That did not deter them from establishing a rich culture of music making in homes, churches, concert halls, and theaters, and they were eager to partake of "music in the genteel tradition" that was imported from Europe and consumed by White America.[13] In the urban centers of the slave states such as Richmond, Virginia; Charleston, South Carolina; and New Orleans, Louisiana, the free Black population tended to be wealthier than their Northern counterparts, while also cultivating a rich and musically literate society. In *The Music of Black Americans: A History*, Eileen Southern writes that New Orleans had the largest Negro population of any American city and was "undoubtedly the most musical city in the land. Sometimes as many as three opera companies were playing at the same time; there were plays and concerts and balls and street parades and, most stirring of all, the yearly celebrations of Carnival or Mardi Gras."[14] She continues to describe the vocal music scene of that city: "At the opera houses, segregated sections were reserved for free Negroes and for slaves. Visitors to the city were surprised to note that even the slaves hummed operatic arias as they walked through the streets."[15] So despite strict racial segregation, Black Americans—enslaved or free—participated in a common musical culture with White Americans and partook of a shared soundscape that was filled with imported European art music as well as folk song from other immigrant populations. In the next section, we will examine how White America created and consumed a musical culture beyond these shared European imports, developing a genre of entertainment based on the denigration of African Americans that would come to epitomize the "American" sound worldwide, cementing and exporting racial stereotypes through popular musical culture for centuries to come.

Antebellum White Americans and the Origins of Blackface Minstrelsy

If you were White and middle to upper class in the nineteenth century, you could gain access to musical training and go to concerts and operas in theaters that featured the imported art music of Europe, which was the highest form of culture. Whites from all classes attended comic revues, or variety shows that featured a range of acts, from bawdy comedy to opera choruses. It was in one of these revues in the 1830s that Thomas Dartmouth Rice, a White New Yorker performing in Pittsburgh, Pennsylvania, made his debut wearing Blackface makeup and shabby clothes and singing "Jump Jim Crow" in a performance that mocked African Americans and played on White stereotypes of slaves.[16] What began that night as one comic sketch in a revue metastasized over the course of the nineteenth century to its own evening of entertainment, featuring a troupe of stock characters played by White performers in Blackface makeup. Beginning in the 1840s, for almost a century, the Blackface minstrel show was by far and away the most popular stage entertainment in America, and "Jump Jim Crow" was the first great international song hit of American popular music. According to popular song historian Charles Hamm, Thomas Dartmouth ("Daddy") Rice was "the first native-born American musician to carry across the Atlantic a type of music recognized abroad as characteristically American,"[17] and the Blackface minstrel show as a genre was also the first form of entertainment that the United States exported to other countries. There are many resources to which one can turn to read about the particulars of Blackface, or "Ethiopian," minstrelsy, but for our purposes, it suffices to say that from almost the very beginning, American musical identity at home and abroad was enmeshed with slavery and its White, dominant culture's fascination with and subjugation of African Americans.

In terms of the music, early minstrel shows did not feature songs created by African Americans, but rather crude facsimiles of musical stereotypes.[18] Instruments associated with "slaves on the plantation" were featured, such as the banjo (which actually did originate in Africa and was introduced to the New World by the enslaved population), the fiddle (a European stringed instrument used in American folk music of Scottish and Irish origins), and the bones (a rhythm instrument of Irish folk origin). White songwriters provided the melodies, although because of their proximity to Black creators, the extent to which any Black source material was absorbed by those songwriters is difficult to quantify. In *The Music of Black Americans: A History*, Eileen

Southern includes a fascinating quote from an 1845 article in *Knickerbocker Magazine* that speaks of the "relationship between minstrel materials and the songs and dances of the slaves":

> Who are our true rulers? The Negro poets, to be sure. Do they not set the fashion, and give laws to the public taste? Let one of them, in the swamps of Carolina, compose a new song, and it no sooner reaches the ear of a white amateur, than it is written down, amended (that is, almost spoilt), printed, and then put upon a course of rapid dissemination, to cease only with the utmost bounds of Anglo-Saxondom, perhaps with the world. Meanwhile, the poor author digs away with his hoe, utterly ignorant of his greatness.[19]

As the author from 1845 (J. Kinnard) points out, it is the White songwriter that profits because of his ability to publish, an avenue that was unavailable to the Black creator before the Civil War. One such White composer of early minstrel songs stands out as the most influential songwriter in American history: Stephen Foster.

Stephen Collins Foster (1826–1864) was born in Lawrenceville, Pennsylvania, on July 4, 1826, and was the first American composer who earned his living from writing and selling his songs. Like Thomas Dartmouth Rice, he was a Northerner, which ironically makes the two most famous pioneers of Blackface minstrelsy, responsible for propagating myths and stereotypes of plantation life in the South, Yankees. (This irony is one that would be repeated in the Tin Pan Alley years at the turn of the twentieth century and well after.) Foster's early association with the first famous minstrel troupe, the Christy Minstrels, as well as the generally better quality of his music, was responsible for the huge success of such songs as "Oh, Susanna," "Nelly Bly," and "Camptown Races." Many of his songs make use of the typical heavy dialect and nonsense lyrics of minstrel songs, but Foster also wrote songs with melodies and texts that carried sincere emotion—such as "Old Uncle Ned" and "Nelly was a lady"—that were the first of their ilk to show the enslaved in a humanizing light.[20] Foster's most popular song during his lifetime was "Old Folks at Home," which expressed the emotions of the Black protagonist rather than mocking him; it also struck a chord with White Americans in the 1850s, many of whom were immigrants who had left families behind in the old country or were leaving their eastern roots for Western expansion. It is interesting to note that "Old Folks at Home" was published in 1851, the same year that the influential novel by abolitionist Harriet Beecher Stowe, *Uncle Tom's Cabin*, appeared in newspapers in serial form[21]; although the song was instrumental in establishing the commercial trope of the old slave longing for the plantation, it also could have, like the novel, helped to move the White dial of empathy toward compassion for the enslaved and support for the abolitionist movement. Therefore, the legacy of Stephen Foster's output reflects and, in some ways, defines the complicated racial dynamics of nineteenth-century antebellum American popular song, and because of their ubiquity and popularity, the songs continue to echo through our cultural subconscious today. Through a study of Foster's oeuvre, we could confront the role that popular song played at the nexus of culture and race in the nineteenth century as well as reflect on the power of popular song, on the one hand, to shape expectations through the commodification of racial stereotypes, and on the other, to elicit emotions that connect us all as human beings.

Emancipation and Reconstruction

The end of the Civil War brought with it massive changes in American society, and we think it's safe to say that our society has yet to come to terms with the ramifications of those changes even today. With a Black underclass now ostensibly free to determine its own fate, African Americans' first order of business was to pursue education, economic advancement, and political representation. Despite the ferocious headwinds of racial segregation and staggering inequity, African Americans began to get college educations, either at liberal Northern institutions such as Oberlin College in Ohio and New England Conservatory in Boston, Massachusetts, or at colleges established by the federal government or missionary groups throughout the South expressly for the education of African Americans, who were not allowed to enroll in the Southern land grant colleges because of the Southern states' racially discriminatory laws meant to keep its Black population separate and subjugated. Now known as HBCU's (historically Black colleges and universities), their role in educating a post-war Black intelligentsia cannot be overstated, with such influential graduates as Booker T. Washington and W.E.B. Du Bois. It is at Du Bois' alma mater, Fisk University in Nashville, Tennessee, where the story of Black voices and Black song (as opposed to White facsimiles) as a marker of American musical identity begins.

Fisk University opened its doors in Nashville, Tennessee in 1866, and its student body was made up of the formerly enslaved from the surrounding area. Musical instruction was offered by White faculty member and treasurer of the university George L. White, and he formed a small choral ensemble from among the student body. Because of financial need, in 1871 Professor White decided to take his nine-member choir on a concert tour to raise funds for the university. The concert program consisted of standard classical repertoire, and the singing was of very high quality, according to newspaper reports, which also recounted the audiences' surprise at seeing African American singers perform with such musical refinement and taste. Before the tour, the student singers never revealed to their professor that they gathered in secret to sing spirituals, remnants of their enslavement that they publicly wished to leave behind but that still brought them solace. But when Professor White heard them sing the spirituals, he understood their power and uniqueness; when the concert tour wasn't generating the money he had hoped to earn, he suggested adding a few spirituals to their program in hopes that their novelty would draw a larger audience. Suffice it to say, the gambit was successful, and the newly renamed "Fisk Jubilee Singers" set off an international clamor to hear "authentic" Black song as opposed to the "base counterfeits"[22] popularized by Blackface minstrelsy.[23] The Fisk Jubilee Singers were responsible for introducing "slave songs" to the White Northern population in the United States and to audiences in Europe as well, performing for President Ulysses S. Grant at the White House in 1872 and for Queen Victoria in England in 1873. The tour raised enough money for Fisk University to build its first permanent building, and the group continued to tour for many years after, inspiring a flood of imitators and a vast market for Negro choruses to populate lavish, large-scale stage productions of *Uncle Tom's Cabin* and plantation tableaux, which were all the rage in the late nineteenth century. Thus, one avenue was opened for African American performers to earn a living with their singing.

Other professional avenues to performing for White audiences began to open as well, as more African American singers gained classical training. The Hyers Sisters, Anna Madah (soprano) and Emma Louise (contralto), toured as a family act and sang on some of the same concerts as the Fisk Jubilee Singers. They ushered in an era of popularity for Black "prima donnas" such as Selika Williams ("Queen of Staccato") and Sissieretta Jones ("The Black Patti"), who sang operatic repertoire in traveling vaudeville troupes as well as for concert audiences in the United States and around the world.[24] But the most reliable form of employment for African American performers, ironically, remained in the Blackface minstrel shows, which by this time had morphed into an evening of family entertainment that eventually developed into vaudeville. When Black performers took the stage, both before and after Emancipation, they were constrained to "put on the costume" of stereotypical Blackness[25] in order to conform to the caricatures that were the stock in trade of "Ethiopian" minstrelsy, which still enjoyed worldwide popularity after the Civil War, and offered the most lucrative of careers in music. One such talented African American performer and songwriter who donned Blackface makeup and made his career on the minstrel stage in the late nineteenth century was James Bland (1854–1911), another Northerner by birth (Flushing, New York) who was descended from freedmen on both sides of his family. His impact on American popular song, in the form of music for minstrel shows, as well as his career trajectory of great success followed by a descent into poverty engendered the obvious comparison to Stephen Foster's biography even during his lifetime, when he was hailed as "The Prince of Negro Songwriters" and proclaimed "one of the three best American composers (the other two were Foster and Sousa)"[26] on one of his many European tours. His most famous songs were written early in his career and include two that are no doubt familiar: the pseudospiritual "Oh, Dem Golden Slippers," and the sentimental plantation ballad "Carry Me Back to Old Virginny." In fact, the latter was so beloved that Virginia made "Carry Me Back to Old Virginny" its state song in 1940 and remarkably, it retained that place of honor until 1997, when it was retired after several re-workings of the lyrics failed to erase the racist taint of their minstrel roots. The song employs a continuation of the same trope that Stephen Foster used in "Old Folks at Home," that of the old slave "longing for the days before the war,"[27] a theme of nostalgia for and romanticizing of the antebellum South that Black Virginians most assuredly did not share, and which would remain a staple of American popular song well into the 1950s.

Confronting the fact that, in the nineteenth century, America established its unique cultural identity by exploiting African Americans as a target of ridicule and a source of profit and that its remnants persist in our culture today is a daunting but vitally important task in addressing current ambivalence on the part of singers of all races who undertake to perform American popular music as well as classic song and spiritual settings by African American composers. But there is power in naming that original act of cultural distortion and economic subjugation, and through the pursuit of a musical "truth and reconciliation,"[28] we can begin to truly pay homage to the voices of nineteenth-century African American creators who fought for their humanity to be heard in their music.

Notes

1. For an interesting discussion of this phenomenon, see *Dvořák's Prophecy* by Joe Horowitz (citation in "Selected Bibliography and Resources").

2. Mellonee Burnim and Portia Maultsby, *African American Music: An Introduction*, second edition (New York: Routledge, 2015), 3.

3. Burnim and Maultsby, *African American Music*, 25.
4. Burnim and Maultsby, *African American Music*, 42.
5. "The Making of African American Identity: Volume 1, 1500-1865," The National Humanities Center, accessed January 9, 2023, http://nationalhumanitiescenter.org/pds/maai/identity/text3/text3read.htm#:~:text=Free%20blacks%20comprised%20about%2011,226%2C000)%20lived%20in%20free%20states.
6. Randye Jones, *So You Want to Sing Spirituals* (Lanham: Rowman & Littlefield, 2019), 4–5.
7. Ben Zehavi, "19th-Century Slave Bible That Removed Exodus Story to Repress Hope Goes on Display," *Times of Israel*, March 29, 2019, https://www.timesofisrael.com/19th-cent-slave-bible-that-removed-exodus-story-to-repress-hope-goes-on-display/.
8. Hansonia Caldwell, *African American Music: A Chronology: 1619-1995* (Los Angeles, CA: Ikoro Communications, 1995), 29–30.
9. Bryan Greene, "When Opera Star Jenny Lind Came to America, She Witnessed a Nation Torn Apart over Slavery," *Smithsonian Magazine*, October 6, 2020, https://www.smithsonianmag.com/history/jenny-lind-swedish-opera-star-slavery-180975990/.
10. Eileen Southern, *The Music of Black Americans: A History*, third edition (New York: W.W. Norton & Company, 1997), 103–04.
11. Southern, *The Music of Black Americans*, 249–50.
12. Ira Berlin, "Free Blacks, 1619-1860," Encyclopedia.com, accessed November 13, 2022, https://www.encyclopedia.com/history/encyclopedias-almanacs-transcripts-and-maps/free-blacks-1619-1860.
13. Southern, *The Music of Black Americans*, 101.
14. Southern, *The Music of Black Americans*, 131–32.
15. Southern, *The Music of Black Americans*, 132.
16. Charles Hamm, *Yesterdays: Popular Song in America* (New York: W.W. Norton & Company, 1979), 118–21.
17. Hamm, *Yesterdays*, 121.
18. Hamm, *Yesterdays*, 121.
19. Southern, *The Music of Black Americans*, fn93.
20. Hamm, *Yesterdays*, 209–12.
21. Hamm, *Yesterdays*, 215.
22. Southern, *The Music of Black Americans*, fn93.
23. For a gripping and detailed account of this concert tour, see *Spirituals and the Birth of a Black Entertainment Industry* by Sandra Jean Graham, chapters 2 and 3.
24. Southern, *The Music of Black Americans*, 244–47.
25. Wesley Morris, "The Birth of American Music," *NY Times* audio series, *1619*, podcast episode #3, September 6, 2019, https://www.nytimes.com/2019/09/06/podcasts/1619-black-american-music-appropriation.html.

26. David Jasen and Gene Jones, *Spreadin' Rhythm Around: Black Popular Songwriters, 1880-1930* (New York: Schirmer Books, 1998), 11.

27. Jasen and Jones, *Spreadin' Rhythm Around*, 9.

28. A reference to the South African Truth and Reconciliation Commission, formed in 1995 to heal the nation after the era of apartheid government. See Desmond Tutu, "Truth and Reconciliation Commission, South Africa," Britannica.com, accessed November 25, 2022, https://www.britannica.com/topic/Truth-and-Reconciliation-Commission-South-Africa.

CHAPTER TWO

The Early Twentieth Century

Race, Music, Popular Culture, and the Harlem Renaissance

A Curated Early Twentieth-Century Timeline[1]

1900: James Weldon Johnson writes "Lift Ev'ry Voice and Sing," the poem later set to music by his brother, J. Rosamond Johnson, that would be promoted by the National Association for the Advancement of Colored People as the Negro National Anthem
- Scott Joplin and Arthur Marshall publish ragtime composition, "Swipsey Cake Walk"

1903: *In Dahomey*, musical by Will Marion Cook and Paul Laurence Dunbar
- *The Souls of Black Folk* by W.E.B. Du Bois

1908: Pace & Handy Music Company founded in Memphis, Tennessee

1909: National Association for the Advancement of Colored People established by a multiracial group of intellectuals and philanthropists

1910: First wireless radio broadcast (from the Metropolitan Opera, featuring the operatic tenor Enrico Caruso)

1912–1915: James Reese Europe and the Clef Club Orchestra perform concerts at Carnegie Hall annually, with a program of music by Black composers to raise funds for the Music School Settlement for Colored People

1914: W.C. Handy publishes "St. Louis Blues" (the most recorded song from 1900–1950[2])

1917: H.T. Burleigh publishes his first volume of spiritual settings

1919: The National Association of Negro Musicians is established in Chicago
1921: *Shuffle Along*, musical by Eubie Blake and Noble Sissle
1921–1923: Black Swan Records founded by Harry Pace
- originally intended to record classical music
- owned by and produced recordings by Black artists
- popular music (especially jazz and blues)
- William Grant Still is musical director
- recordings disseminate Black song to majority White population without the burdens of segregated live performance, proving that there is a universal audience for Black song

1924: Gershwin premieres *Rhapsody in Blue*, commissioned by and performed with Paul Whiteman and His Concert Orchestra in Aeolian Hall in New York

1927: *Showboat*, musical by Jerome Kern and Oscar Hammerstein II
- Duke Ellington and the Cotton Club Orchestra begin their weekly national radio broadcasts

1931: Premiere of *Afro-American Symphony* (*Symphony #1*) by William Grant Still; first symphony written by an African American to be performed by a major symphony orchestra (Rochester Philharmonic)

1932: Florence Price and Margaret Bonds take top prizes for symphony and song categories in the Wanamaker Competition for Negro Composers

1933: Margaret Bonds, pianist and composer, is first Black soloist with a major symphony orchestra (performed *Concertino for piano and orchestra* by John Alden Carpenter)[3]
- Hall Johnson's music-drama, *Run, Little Chillun'*, premieres on Broadway with the Hall Johnson Negro Choir; first play with an African American director and composer to appear on Broadway

1934: The Apollo Theater opens as a venue for Black performers and patrons; Ella Fitzgerald's career is launched there the same year
- 60 percent of American homes have radios
- William Dawson's *Negro Folk Symphony* premiered at Carnegie Hall with the Philadelphia Orchestra conducted by Leopold Stokowski

1935: *Porgy and Bess* opens at the Alvin Theater on Broadway

1936: *Billy the Kid* (ballet) by Aaron Copland

1939: Marian Anderson sings concert at the Lincoln Memorial

1940: *Symphony #3* of Florence Price (commissioned by Works Progress Administration, written in 1938) premieres at the Detroit Institute of Art by the Detroit Civic Orchestra conducted by Valter Poole

1940: Playwright Abram Hill and actor Frederick O'Neal found the American Negro Theatre
1943: *Black, Brown and Beige*, jazz symphony by Duke Ellington, his first concert at Carnegie Hall
1944: *Appalachian Spring*, one-act ballet by Aaron Copland, premieres at the Library of Congress

The Promise of a New Century: The Pursuit of Education, Respect, and Economic Autonomy

The turn of the twentieth century was a period of great optimism for African Americans, as it was for the country as a whole. With educational opportunities, albeit mostly segregated, opening avenues of intellectual and economic advancement, there was a striving among African Americans to attain the dominant culture's ideals of dignity and respectability that belied hopes of entering American culture and society as equals. W.E.B. Du Bois' call to the "Talented Tenth" of the Negro population was a quest to "identify and empower those African Americans of exceptional ability"[4] through education and the pursuit of high culture, while Booker T. Washington focused on the acquisition of vocational skills to ensure African American economic independence. In terms of musical attainment, African American composers and musicians were finally able to get the rigorous musical training that they hoped would lead to careers in classical music, as opposed to being consigned to careers as Ethiopian minstrels, thereby demonstrating their cultural equality and dignity. These African American aspirations were part of a widespread societal desire for moral and intellectual uplift that inspired the pursuit of high culture and fueled the search for an American voice in classical music.

Through the patronage of the wealthiest members of the Gilded Age elite, cultural institutions were being established in major cities around the country (e.g., Boston Symphony Orchestra, 1881; Metropolitan Opera, 1883; Chicago Symphony Orchestra, 1889), and in 1885, philanthropist Jeannette Meyers Thurber was led by her desire to develop a "national musical spirit"[5] to establish the National Conservatory of Music. The school had a progressive mission to train the most talented musicians regardless of race, gender, disability, or financial means. Perhaps it was this pursuit of a "national musical spirit" that led her to hire Antonin Dvořák (1841–1904), a world-famous composer of the Nationalist school, to lead the conservatory, which he did from 1892–1895. Dvořák was a Bohemian composer who based much of his musical inspiration on the folk music of his homeland, and his position at the National Conservatory brought him into contact with H.T. Burleigh, an African American student who would become an important inspiration for Dvořák's composition during his time in the United States. Burleigh (1866–1949) was the grandson of a slave and grew up hearing spirituals, and these folk songs forged from the crucible of enslavement were a revelation to Dvořák. When he heard Burleigh sing these "negro melodies," Dvořák became convinced that they "must be the real foundation of any serious and original school of composition to be developed in the United States."[6] Dvořák soaked up inspiration from every corner of the American soundscape and wrote what is arguably one of the most beloved and performed symphonic compositions of all time, his *9th Symphony ("From the New World")*, which premiered in 1893 in New York. The plaintive main theme of its second movement is clearly an homage to Burleigh and the sorrow songs that he sang for his teacher. Burleigh reciprocated by carrying his teacher's nationalistic compositional vision forward with his groundbreaking concert arrangements of Negro spirituals and went on to become the first African American to "achieve national distinction as a composer, arranger, and concert artist."[7]

Like the example of Dvořák and Burleigh, White and Black musicians and audiences began to interact in a more substantive way at this moment in history, and a Black professional class of musicians navigated the many challenges for African Americans, taking advantage of new technology and popular fads while meeting the demands of the White public for their "exotic" music and dancing. After an early experience in which W.C. Handy was duped out of the commercial rights to one of the first songs he had published, he founded the Pace & Handy Music Company in 1908 with his friend Harry Pace, thereby establishing one of the first Black-owned music publishing houses. Taking control over his future profits would serve him very well, since his next big song hit was "St. Louis Blues," which has the distinction of being one of the most influential popular songs in American history,[8] ushering in a profitable craze for "the Blues," and which would provide the impetus for future genres of Black music, such as jazz and rock and roll, that would come to define American music writ large.

As in the case of W.C. Handy, economic autonomy was a major goal for African Americans at this moment in history because the community faced practically insurmountable barriers in terms of employment and equitable pay. For example, there was a musician's union in New York, but it didn't accept Black players, so they were inevitably paid much less than their White counterparts, if at all. But one enterprising band leader, composer, and arranger, James Reese Europe, had a plan to remedy that problem, and he leveraged his own personal reputation, skills, and relationships to single handedly ensure a stable market for his fellow African American musicians when he established the Clef Club in 1910. The Clef Club functioned like a musician's union that negotiated guaranteed standard pay for well-trained (and well-dressed) musicians who were in great demand all over New York city for parties, clubs, and dance bands. In time, the Clef Club became a byword for high-quality music provided by skilled Black musicians, in large part due to the notoriety James Reese Europe gained from leading the band for Irene and Vernon Castle, the dancing couple who set the trends for the wildly popular ballroom dancing craze of the teens, when the foxtrot was born.[9] The Clef Club Orchestra also played the first concerts at Carnegie Hall consisting of a program of music by Black composers. The first such concert, in 1912, included works by Europe himself, as well as "songs by J. Rosamond Johnson and Will Marion Cook, a new spiritual by Harry Burleigh, Samuel Coleridege-Taylor's 'By the Waters of Babylon,' . . . and, to show that a Black singer and orchestra could handle the classics, an aria from Saint-Saens' *Samson and Delilah.*"[10] The Clef Club played to a packed, integrated audience that night, proving that the "idea of African Americans making 'serious' music would never seem ridiculous again."[11]

Interracial Collaborations and the Birth of a Music Economy Based on Black Music

With the advent of the recording industry and the new technology of radio, it was much easier for White audiences to hear the music of Black artists and composers (from both popular and classical genres of music) since those new modes of music consumption could bypass the barrier of audience segregation. When his partnership with W.C. Handy dissolved, Harry Pace started the Pace Phonograph Company, the first Black-owned record company, and called it "Black Swan Records," in honor of Elizabeth Taylor Greenfield. Black Swan Records was originally intended to record classical music performed by Black artists, but soon began to capitalize on the blues craze, featuring artists such as Ethel Waters, and also gave aspiring musicians such as William Grant Still (who worked as an arranger for the label) a start. The records Black Swan produced were called "race records" and were aimed at the African American buying public, but they were purchased widely by White customers as well, possibly because elements of Black vernacular music such as syncopation and blue notes had long since been absorbed into the songs emanating from Tin Pan Alley that were beloved by Americans of all races. At the same time that Black music was having such a profound effect on American culture, with ragtime, blues, and jazz dominating popular music, there was an interracial community taking action, attempting to create a path to equality for African Americans. The National Association for the Advancement of Colored People was established in 1909 as a demonstration of this community, and White and Black musicians formed one as well when they came into contact in the heady creative milieu of the Harlem Renaissance.

As a result of the terrible conditions for African Americans in the South, with laws limiting practically every aspect of their existence, and subject to horrific violence or death in the form of lynching if they broke either written or unwritten codes of behavior, vast numbers of African Americans moved to the North and Midwest to urban centers, where they could escape Jim Crow and find better paying jobs. As a result of this so-called Great Migration, African American populations in these urban centers increased exponentially in a short period of time, creating a market for Black entertainments of all sorts. Concurrently, African American intellectuals gravitated to New York as a center of Black culture, with a desire to organize for the goal of equality, racial uplift, and creative expression, and this concentration of creative genius resulted in an outpouring of music, poetry, novels, plays, and social activism that is known as the Harlem Renaissance. The Harlem Renaissance took off in the Roaring Twenties, an era known for its high spirits and conviviality (despite, or possibly because of, Prohibition), and lasted for roughly fifteen years, but there was so much Black music happening in a setting where music was the currency of social interaction—live bands played for dance halls, nightclubs, Broadway shows, and radio shows—that Black and White composers and musicians were all imbibing the same sounds and energy. There remained racial realities that had to be navigated, such as the fact that White musicians had no problem entering Black spaces to hear music, but interracial gatherings rarely happened the other way around. For example, Black performers and musicians comprised the entire company of the show at Harlem's Cotton Club, but African Americans were not allowed in the all-White audience.[12] However, there was a notable exception to this one-way street, and that was at the parties given by Carl Van Vechten, who is credited in the *Encyclopedia of the Harlem Renaissance* as being one of the most influential figures of that movement. Van Vechten befriended many of the luminaries of the Harlem Renaissance, such as James Weldon Johnson and Langston Hughes, to name just two, and used his "considerable influence in New York to promote African American writers and artists."[13] He hosted parties in his home where some of the most high-profile Black performers of the age—such as Paul Robeson, Josephine Baker, and Ethel Waters, who couldn't stay in certain hotels because of their race—were included on the guest list, not the kitchen staff. Many legendary artists crossed paths at these interracial parties, and the relationship of two of them, both pianists and composers, would prove to be one of the most consequential in the development of American music, that of James P. Johnson (1894–1955) and George Gershwin (1898–1937).

Johnson and Gershwin had so much in common that it's not surprising they became friends. They were both pianists of extraordinary ability, composers of show tunes and of music for the concert hall, and foundational to the establishing of jazz as a genre that could unite both the popular and classical worlds. Their paths crossed many times in the professional world as well as at Van Vechten's parties, but they first met when they were both making piano rolls for the Aeolian company.[14] (Piano rolls produced for player pianos were a form of music distribution that coincided with the early recording industry and captured the performances of many legendary pianists of the era.) Johnson was the "father of stride piano," a style of piano playing that arose from ragtime, but because its hallmark is the virtuosity of its practitioners, it never entered the consumer market of published sheet music for amateur players, and much of his solo piano music remains obscure today. However, James P. Johnson's song legacy is still very much alive with his iconic music that is now synonymous with the "Charleston" dance. According to Margaret Moos Pick, a prominent radio producer for *Riverwalk Jazz*, a public radio program that celebrates early jazz recordings, "George Gershwin acknowledged his high esteem for Johnson and the enormous influence Johnson's work had on his own by including the 'Charleston' theme in his *Concerto in F*."[15] Both Johnson and Gershwin studied composition over the course of their careers, and "in 1928, four years after Gershwin presented his first serious work, *Rhapsody in Blue*, Johnson debuted his first symphonic work in concert at Carnegie Hall with Fats Waller at the piano."[16] *Yamekraw, A Negro Rhapsody*, was a dazzling demonstration of African American musical excellence:

> In the presentation and performance of *Yamekraw*, a rhapsody for symphony orchestra and piano, James P. Johnson and Thomas "Fats" Waller teamed up with William Grant Still and W.C. Handy in a performance that surely satisfied the intellectuals. Composed by Johnson, orchestrated by Still, conducted by Handy, with the piano solo played by Waller, the piece employed "spirituals and blues tunes," among others, and was played in that performance by a symphony orchestra made up of Harlem musicians. This was Renaissance style—exactly in keeping with the dreams and goals of Renaissance leadership and masses.[17]

The title of Johnson's piece makes the connection to Gershwin's quite clear: *Yamekraw, a Negro Rhapsody*.[18] In this ambitious concert piece dedicated to a Black community near Savannah, Georgia, called Yamekraw, "you can hear strains of down-home blues, stomps, church meetings and spirituals,"[19] the same strains that Gershwin would go on to employ in his opera *Porgy and Bess* in 1935. And whereas Gershwin is now rightly recognized for his contributions to concert music that have remained some of the most popular in the repertory, James P. Johnson's "achievements never translated into celebrity for him."[20] And it is this divergence that defines just one of the many barriers Black composers faced as they sought recognition and acceptance in the music economy of the early twentieth century.

Reality Sets In: Barriers from Stereotypes, Segregation, and Jim Crow

Depending on your perspective, from our vantage point one hundred years hence, it may or may not be hard to imagine a world in which the denigration of African Americans was so pervasive. For African Americans who escaped Jim Crow, their reality in cities of the North and Midwest included redlining and ghetto-ized neighborhoods, disparities in pay and job opportunities, and continued segregation in many public spaces. Popular music and stage productions perpetuated demeaning stereotypes left over from Blackface minstrelsy and added some new ones to the mix. One turn-of-the-century innovation was called the "coon" song, that invariably cast the Black man as a fast-living, vain, dangerous character; another strain of popular song wallowed in nostalgia for an imaginary "Southland" that always smelled of magnolia blossoms wafted on warm breezes (as in "The Birth of the Blues" from *George White's Scandals of 1926*); others made references to Southern happy "darkies" and their carefree dancing (as in the 1927 hit "Mississippi Mud" recorded by Bing Crosby with Paul Whiteman's Rhythm Boys). It is the height of irony to consider that these tropes were perpetuated by mostly White Tin Pan Alley songwriters who had never been to the South; it is also ironic that because these songs were so popular, the tropes became solidified and self-perpetuating in American culture. Black show music composers responded to these limitations by innovating their way into a White market saturated with operetta and vaudeville; they pioneered a dynamic new style of show featuring Black dance styles, in which beautiful chorus girls executed fast-paced, energetic choreography, thereby showcasing Black talent, and creating a demand for their vernacular-inspired performance that would transform American musical theatre. The show that pioneered this transformation was *Shuffle Along*, which premiered in 1921 and was created by Black writers (Noble Sissle and Eubie Blake) and performed by an all-Black cast, and its long-running popularity launched the careers of several future legendary artists. Shows that emulated that formula proliferated (*Keep Shufflin'*, *Runnin' Wild*, *Chocolate Dandies*, *Hot Chocolates*), but eventually became straightjackets that consigned African American performers to replicating representations of exotic, primitive ("jungle music"), or sexualized Blackness. And because these images defined Blackness for the dominant culture (in addition to the persistent racist minstrel stereotypes), the idea that African Americans would be capable of writing and performing classical music was a cognitive dissonance that was difficult to reconcile for those in the world of "refined" arts. Joseph Horowitz defines this era's bifurcation in his book, *Dvořák's Prophecy*: "the smart syncopations of [Joplin's] rags, their physicality and steady energy—led in two directions: jazz and the concert hall. For Black musicians the first direction was by far the more productive. The result . . . was a high/low schism more pronounced (and of course more racial) than any such musical schism abroad. Popular music was Black; classical music was White."[21]

In defiance of this schism, two important African American pioneers of classical singing demonstrated the power of concert music as a marker of dignity like the Fisk Jubilee Singers before them. Roland Hayes (1887–1976) and Marian Anderson (1902–1993), who came of age during the Harlem Renaissance, exemplified not only the barriers that Black classical musicians faced, but also the importance of the vocal performer to overcoming those barriers. According to Eileen Southern, "to the Black communities that helped them to rise, the Black concert artists who achieved distinction during the Harlem Renaissance were more than just talented and successful individuals. They became race symbols, whose successes were shared vicariously by the great mass of Black Americans that could never hope to attain similar distinction."[22] Because opera companies were segregated, Hayes and Anderson had no hope of making their careers on the major opera stages of the world, but they were able to gain worldwide prominence as concert artists, appearing either in solo recitals or with major orchestras. Both Hayes and Anderson were met with indifference when they first began performing in the United States, and it was only after they were received with great acclaim in Europe—Hayes gave a command performance for King George V in 1921—that they were able to return home and command audiences as well as respect. In 1935, when the legendary conductor Arturo Toscanini heard Marian Anderson sing a recital in Salzburg, Austria, he told her, "Yours is a voice such as one hears once in a hundred years," and by 1941, Anderson "was one of the ten highest-paid concert artists in the United States."²³ She was at the height of her fame when the Daughters of the American Revolution refused to let her perform at Constitution Hall in Washington, DC, because of her race, which provided the opportunity for a much greater achievement: a concert, facilitated with the help of First Lady Eleanor Roosevelt, on the steps of the Lincoln Memorial on Easter Sunday 1939, before an audience of seventy-five thousand people.²⁴

The New Negro and Vocal Concert Music

Roland Hayes and Marian Anderson demonstrated the characteristics of courage, flexibility, and persistence that all African American musicians of that era had to draw on if they were to realize their dreams of performing classical music. In the Black community, mentorship and intra-group support was a sustaining force, and "any artist who succeeded in breaking down a color barrier inspired other talented Black men and women to overcome almost insurmountable difficulties."²⁵ Historically Black colleges and universities (HBCUs) represented possibly the most important source of education and mentorship for this generation of composers and musicians, given how many prominent artists (such as Roland Hayes) claim an HBCU as their alma mater. The fact that audiences were segregated also played a role in how African American artists engaged with their racial identity in performance. Eileen Southern contextualizes the reality for Black musicians in the following excerpt:

> Black performers frequently found it important to have Black-music pieces in their repertories—because of segregation, they were performing primarily for Black audiences, and they wanted to be able to communicate with their listeners. Thus the singer sang spirituals or Negro folksongs or music with titles that suggested Negro life and that made obvious use of folklike melodies and rhythms. The dance-music composer utilized boogie-woogie rhythms, the blues, and jazz because Black dancers demanded these musical styles. All this of course did not excuse Black performers from developing classical music repertories. They simply had to learn both–the African American and the European.²⁶

But since the Harlem Renaissance (also known as the New Negro movement), was an intellectual flowering, "a unique awakening of mind and spirit, of race consciousness and artistic advancement,"²⁷ Black composers aspired to express their African American identity and creativity through concert music and sought to distance themselves from popular culture as the only form of Black musical expression. In the following excerpt, soprano and educator Genithia Hogges describe the values of the New Negro movement:

During the Harlem Renaissance, an elite intelligentsia flourished with artistic grace in the realms of music, visual art, drama, literature, and philosophy. Although today the Harlem Renaissance is virtually equated with the Jazz Age, at the time of its inception, jazz culture (an amalgam of music, dance, and social behaviors) was condemned by the self-selected agenda setters of the African American community. Renowned thinkers and editors of the time (the likes of Alain Locke) demeaned jazz as base music, preferring to focus attention on the classically-oriented musical compositions of African American artists—art songs, concertized spirituals, oratorios, and substantial choral and instrumental works by Florence Price and R. Nathaniel Dett, among others. Indeed, if one looks to writings of the period with regards to African American music, little attention is paid to allegedly untrained and untalented non-art of jazz.[28]

Classic song was a powerful medium for the expression of those values because the New Negro movement produced so much great poetry. Innovative poets proliferated, such as Arna Bontemps, Countee Cullen, and, most notably, Langston Hughes, and African American composers used their powerful poetry to create beautiful and poignant songs with a level of cultural relevance that moved the art form way beyond the parlor songs of the late Victorian age by incorporating social and political commentary in their music. In addition to art songs, composers of the Harlem Renaissance also dedicated themselves to continuing the practice begun by H.T. Burleigh of arranging spirituals in the style of classic song for solo voice and piano accompaniment, and their efforts to honor and preserve this body of song produced a staple of the repertoire for great African American recital singers of this period, from Roland Hayes and Marian Anderson to Paul Robeson and Dorothy Maynor. These songs were typically presented as the last set on the program after the singer had demonstrated their classical bona fides in all the requisite languages, but far from serving as mere "crowd pleasers," they provided a powerful final statement of racial pride and consciousness-raising for audiences. When Marian Anderson ended her recital in Salzburg (the one heard by Toscanini in 1935) with a group of spirituals, one listener described the audience response:

> At the end of the [last] spiritual, there was no applause at all–a silence instinctive, natural, and intense, so that you were afraid to breathe. What Anderson had done was something outside the limits of classical or romantic music: she frightened us with the conception, in musical terms, of course, but outside the normal limits, of a mighty suffering.[29]

Hall Johnson (1888–1970) was one of the many Black composers of the Harlem Renaissance who followed Harry T. Burleigh's example of writing both art songs and arranging spirituals for concert performance, and his biography demonstrates the achievements of its artists, as well as its intellectual aims and African American aesthetics. Johnson was born in Georgia and received some of his early education at HBCUs before going on to earn a bachelor of arts at the University of Pennsylvania. He arrived in New York in 1914 and took part in all the musical opportunities that were open Black musicians at that time, such as playing violin in the groups "led by James Reese Europe that toured with dancers Vernon and Irene Castle,"[30] playing in the pit orchestra for Shuffle Along (which also included William Grant Still playing oboe, incidentally), playing viola as a member of "the Negro String Quartet that appeared with Roland Hayes at Carnegie Hall in 1925,"[31] and composing for the Broadway stage. Although he was an instrumentalist and composer, he revered the power of "Negro singing" and sought to "pour that music into traditional European forms"[32] such as "the art song, the motet and chorus, . . . the music drama, and the operetta or musical comedy."[33] He combined his passion for his African American musical heritage with his classical music training, and, beginning with founding the Hall Johnson Negro Choir in 1925, he devoted himself to vocal music composition and performance for the rest of his career.

More will be said in later chapters about Hall Johnson's achievements as one of the most important proponents of the respectful performance of spiritual arrangements, both solo and choral. But there hardly exists a better example of Harlem Renaissance song writing than Johnson's setting of Langston Hughes' "Mother to Son."

Mother to Son
by Langston Hughes

Well, son, I'll tell you:
Life for me ain't been no crystal stair.
It's had tacks in it,
And splinters,
And boards torn up,
And places with no carpet on the floor—
Bare.
But all the time
I'se been a-climbin' on,
And reachin' landin's,
And turnin' corners,
And sometimes goin' in the dark
Where there ain't been no light.
So boy, don't you turn back.

Don't you set down on the steps
'Cause you finds it's kinder hard.
Don't you fall now—
For I'se still goin', honey,
I'se still climbin',
And life for me ain't been no crystal stair.[34]

The poem is in the first-person voice of a mother trying to encourage her son not to give up in the face of adversity, which is a pretty universal experience. However, Hughes makes it clear through the use of dialect that this is a Black mother talking to her son. If one imagines the dangers, hardships, and humiliation regularly faced by African Americans (men, in particular) in the early twentieth century, the power of her words conveys a stoic determination that has sustained the Black community for centuries. Johnson takes this determination as a starting point, and, with his musical interpretation, draws out and intensifies this moment between mother and son, building to a climax that feels as monumental as Moses and the Ten Commandments. It begins very sparsely, with repeated dotted eighth-sixteenth note thirds hobbling up from the bass in the piano introduction, and when the musical stairs reach the first landing, the mother catches her breath and speaks (see figure 2.1, mm. 1–4).

Figure 2.1. "Mother to Son" (Excerpt A)
Hall, 1888–1970. *The Hall Johnson Collection: Over 50 Classic Favorites for Voice and Piano.* New York: Carl Fischer, 2003.

mm. 22–24

Figure 2.2. "Mother to Son" (Excerpt B)
Hall, 1888–1970. *The Hall Johnson Collection: Over 50 Classic Favorites for Voice and Piano.* New York: Carl Fischer, 2003.

She delivers her opening in a very matter-of-fact way, in a low tessitura, accompanied by regular quarter note thirds rising stepwise through the bass. But in the second section, the minor mode changes to major, the vocal tessitura rises to the top of the staff, and the piano writing becomes more melodic and harmonically lush in the right hand. These compositional choices could signify the mother's hope, and Johnson also interprets an element of optimism in the mother's story with the twinkling sixteenth note flourishes high in the right hand that accompany "where there ain't been no light" (see figure 2.2, mm. 22–24).

But she quickly comes back to the present reality and her rickety staircase to deliver the last part of her message. Over a return to the opening section's deliberate, quarter-note rising motive in the left hand, the mother tells her son seemingly through gritted teeth-teeth in a low tessitura, "don't you set down on the steps 'cause you finds it kinder hard." She continues by tenderly encouraging her son, but then, musically gathering enough strength for the both of them, she repeats the text "I'se still climbin'" five times in rising succession (see figure 2.3, mm. 38–44), ending on a two-measure melisma that climbs and crescendos, buoyed on a wave of pianistic texture reminiscent of Rachmaninoff in a display of epic strength and determination.

This triumphant coda is interrupted by a moment of dissonant, bitter reflection (see figure 2.4, mm. 45–46), but she gathers her determination and tries one more time, reaching the last step of her staircase on the word "life," set to the highest, loudest sustained note of the song (see figure 2.4, m. 47). After this point her strength wanes and the musical energy drains away on a long diminuendo ("life for me") followed by silence (see figure 2.4, mm. 48–51), finishing with the tessitura of both the voice and piano chromatically descending to their lowest levels ("ain't been no crystal stair"), arriving at the tonic of C minor with

mm. 38–44

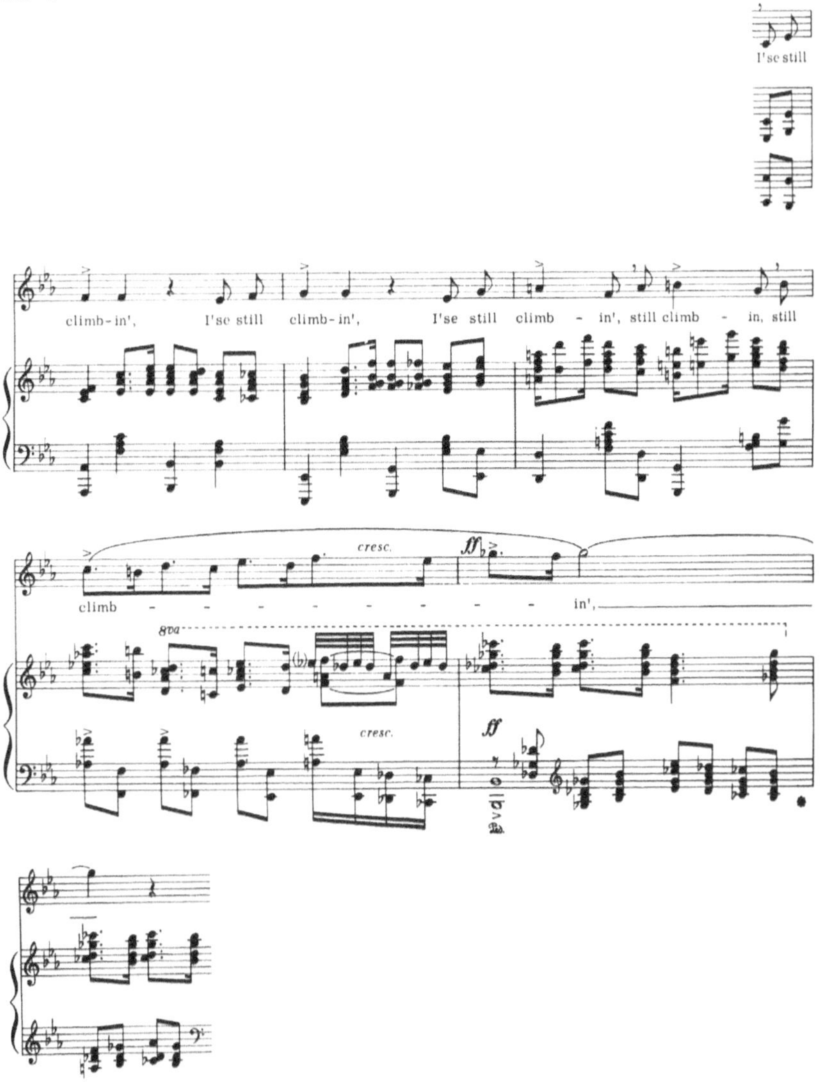

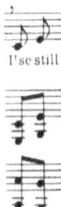

Figure 2.3. "Mother to Son" (Excerpt C)

Hall, 1888–1970. *The Hall Johnson Collection: Over 50 Classic Favorites for Voice and Piano.* New York: Carl Fischer, 2003.

Figure 2.4. "Mother to Son" (Excerpt D)
Hall, 1888–1970. *The Hall Johnson Collection: Over 50 Classic Favorites for Voice and Piano*. New York: Carl Fischer, 2003.

mm. 54–59

Figure 2.5. "Mother to Son" (Excerpt E)
Hall, 1888–1970. *The Hall Johnson Collection: Over 50 Classic Favorites for Voice and Piano.* New York: Carl Fischer, 2003.

the piano striking, repeating, and finally sustaining a low C1 like a foreboding, tolling bell (see figure 2.5, mm. 54–end).

One could and should fill countless recitals exploring the many great voices of the Harlem Renaissance because the truest and most powerful expression of its ideals is to be found in its music. The centrality of vocal music in particular is emphasized by historian Samuel Floyd when he states that "the music of the Black theater shows, the dance music of the cabarets, the blues and ragtime of the speakeasies and the rent parties, the spirituals and the art songs of the recital and concert halls all created an ambiance for Renaissance activity and contemplation."[35] Navigating the popular song and show music repertoire from that era is challenging because of the pervasive, commercialized racism they often perpetuate. But if you look for African American composers and lyricists, you will find songs of great vitality and creativity that often shed a nuanced light on the African American experience of that era, such as "Black and Blue" by Fats Waller and Andy Razaf, featured in *Connie's Hot Chocolates* from 1929. On the classical side, the variety of the repertoire by such composers as J. Rosamond Johnson (1873–1954), R. Nathaniel Dett (1882–1943), Florence Price (1888–1953), and William Grant Still (1895–1978) provide an emotional depth and texture to the information on the pages of history books, allowing students of today to *sing* African American history into the mainstream, in a manner of speaking. Furthermore, through doing the work of studying, practicing, and performing the songs, the creators' experiences come alive for performers and audiences alike, akin to opening a time capsule filled with treasured objects from another time and place.

When we sing songs written from the turn of the century through the Harlem Renaissance, we *feel* what was important to African Americans in that era of optimism, racial pride, and continued struggle. In the next chapter, which takes us into the Civil Rights era and beyond, we will look at how the vocal music of African Americans not only expressed their creative genius, but fundamentally changed American society. As music historian Richard Crawford describes it, "the rise of rock and roll turned the cultural identity of American youth in an interracial direction. The tide that carried rock and rollers to fame was grounded in a process of social change that reached far beyond music."[36]

Notes

1. Picking a topic and creating a curated timeline is an excellent teaching tool for researching the life cycle of a song or the diverse threads of the tapestry of an era. See chapter 8, under the heading "Research Projects."

2. Hamm, *Yesterdays*, 487.

3. There is an interesting account from the Chicago Symphony Archives: (https://csoarchives.wordpress.com/tag/rodman-wanamaker/); Florence Price's *Symphony in E minor* was premiered on the same concert.

4. Sandra L. West and Aberjhani, "Du Bois, W.E.B.," in *Encyclopedia of the Harlem Renaissance* (New York: Checkmark Books, 2003), 90.

5. Emanuel Rubin, "Jeannette Meyers Thurber and the National Conservatory of Music," *American Music* 8, no. 3 (Autumn 1990): 294–325.

6. Southern, *The Music of Black Americans*, 267.

7. Southern, *The Music of Black Americans*, 269.

8. Jasen and Jones, *Spreadin' Rhythm Around*, 235.

9. Jasen and Jones, *Spreadin' Rhythm Around*, 158–64.

10. Jasen and Jones, *Spreadin' Rhythm Around*, 157.

11. Jasen and Jones, *Spreadin' Rhythm Around*, 157.

12. The Cotton Club is where Duke Ellington and his orchestra came to national prominence due to their weekly radio broadcasts. It is problematic to consider the Faustian bargain Ellington and his players had to accept by playing in a segregated environment in order to gain widespread success.

13. Aberjhani, "Van Vechten, Carl," *Encyclopedia of the Harlem Renaissance*, 340.

14. Jasen and Jones, *Spreadin' Rhythm Around*, 376.

15. Margaret Moos Pick, "Runnin' Wild: A Biography of James P. Johnson," The Jim Cullum Riverwalk Jazz Collection (Stanford Archive of Recorded Sound), accessed December 16, 2022, https://riverwalkjazz.stanford.edu/?q=program/runnin-wild-biography-james-p-johnson.

16. Pick, "Runnin' Wild."

17. Samuel Floyd, "Music in the Harlem Renaissance: An Overview," in *Black Music in the Harlem Renaissance: A Collection of Essays*, edited by Samuel Floyd (New York: Greenwood Press, 1990), 15.

18. For an in-depth discussion of this connection, see John Howland, "Jazz Rhapsodies in Black and White: James P. Johnson's 'Yamekraw,'" *American Music* 24, no. 4 (2006): 445–509.

19. Pick, "Runnin' Wild."

20. Jasen and Jones, *Spreadin' Rhythm Around*, 386.

21. Horowitz, *Dvořák's Prophecy*, 18.

22. Southern, *The Music of Black Americans*, 408–09.

23. Southern, *The Music of Black Americans*, 412.

24. "Marian Anderson," *Britannica*, accessed December 17, 2022, https://www.britannica.com/biography/Marian-Anderson.

25. Southern, *The Music of Black Americans*, 409.

26. Southern, *The Music of Black Americans*, 424.

27. West, "Introduction: Black Phoenix Rising," *Encyclopedia of the Harlem Renaissance*, xviii.

28. Lilia Genithia Hogges, "Canonization Reconstructed Inclusion and Exclusion in Nineteeth-Century African American Periodicals with an Ear to the Music of African Americans," *American Periodicals* 12 (2002): 158.

29. Quoted in Southern, *The Music of Black Americans*, 412. Original source: Vincent Sheean, *Between the Thunder and the Sun* (New York, 1943); reprinted in *The Negro in Music and Art*, edited by Lindsay Patterson (Washington, DC, 1967), 158.

30. Southern, *The Music of Black Americans*, 420.

31. West, "Johnson, Hall," *Encyclopedia of the Harlem Renaissance*, 176.

32. Southern, *The Music of Black Americans*, 280.

33. Southern, *The Music of Black Americans*, 280.

34. Song of America, accessed December 19, 2022, https://songofamerica.net/song/mother-to-son/. Source: Langston Hughes, "The Collected Poems of Langston Hughes," edited by Arnold Rampersad and David Roessel (New York: Knopf, 1994).

35. Floyd, "Music in the Harlem Renaissance: An Overview," 3.

36. Richard Crawford, *America's Musical Life: A History* (New York: Norton, 2001), 735.

CHAPTER THREE

Post-War, the Civil Rights Era, and Beyond

Black Music and Its Impact in the Post–World War II Era

If the turn of the century was a time of optimism for African Americans, the post-war era was its inverse, in which African Americans felt frustration and disillusionment. Progress toward true equality was hampered by lack of economic opportunities as well as the resulting poverty of African American communities in urban centers, giving rise to ghettos and the perception that Black neighborhoods were inherently crime-ridden and poor. Meanwhile, Jim Crow was holding strong in the South, which saw a spike in lynchings following the return of Black veterans from fighting for American ideals against Nazism in World War II. In this environment where Black citizens were "free" but White people still had all the power, Black musicians persevered and charted their own paths with their music in three vital streams: jazz, popular song, and concert music.

Jazz: Swing to Bebop

Swing ruled the world of jazz by the early 1940s, dominated by bands led by Count Basie, Duke Ellington, Glenn Miller, and Bennie Goodman. What began as a form created by Black musicians had become the dominant culture's popular music for that generation, performed and enjoyed by White and Black Americans alike. Although there were instances of integration among their musicians, the bands and the audiences were largely segregated, with Black band leaders leading Black players, and White band leaders with their mostly White players garnering more and more success and prominence. Black swing bands were now part of a larger movement that was dictated by White tastes, and this chafed African American jazz musicians, who sought ways to reclaim jazz as a Black art form. Led by Thelonius Monk and Dizzy Gillespie, jazz musicians experimented in small New York clubs in the mid-1940s and pioneered a virtuosic offshoot of jazz called bebop that "made solo improvisation *the* fundamental aspect of jazz performance and the main measure of a performer's standing."[1] Bebop was a declaration of independence from commercial constraints that centered the skill and creativity of individual Black musicians in a closed community. Richard Crawford describes its ethos by saying that "whether in public or on record . . . bebop was a provocative music, performed by a new breed of musician. Rather than courting audience members, beboppers seemed almost eager to separate listeners who 'dug' the music from those who did not."[2]

In the swing era, singers sang songs that were accompanied by the big bands, employing a "soloist-with-orchestra" model that placed an emphasis on the melody, the voice of the singer, and often the singer's glamour. So when the emphasis of jazz moved to improvisation, which was an instrumental concept, singers found a way to adapt using sounds and syllables drawn from the text as well as their musical imaginations to become vocal instrumentalists. "Scat singing" as a practice was not new to African American singers and had been employed across many genres since at least the turn of the century, with Cab Calloway being a prominent example during the swing era. But bebop singers took this style of improvisation and refined it to more than just entertaining "riffing." They imbued their extended scat solos with rhythmic and percussive vitality through the choice of their vowels and consonants; they explored complex harmonies in linear form with perfect intonation and expressive articulation; and they unleashed their musical imaginations with melodic quotations ranging from classical tunes to nursery rhymes. Sarah Vaughan (1924–1990) was one of the great bebop singers who came on the scene in the 1940s, and in his book, *America's Musical Life: A History*, Richard Crawford quotes jazz scholar Martin Williams on the example of her impact and achievements:

> with Vaughan's arrival on the scene in the 1940s, "without formal training but with a voice of exceptional range, body, volume and variety of vocal textures," to which she added excellent control, plus an ear and sense of pitch that "were just about perfect." . . . The essay ends with a tribute that places Vaughan's work in a context beyond jazz, popular music, or American music: she is seen as a contributor to the history of singing. "It took several generations of singers in the seventeenth- and eighteenth-century Italy to explore the potential of the

human voice and arrive at what we call the *bel canto* style," Williams writes. "Sarah Vaughan accomplished the virtual equivalent of those explorations in a contemporary American style, in less than one lifetime, and in a single voice."[3]

The breathtaking musicianship and vocal skill of singers such as Sarah Vaughan and Ella Fitzgerald is not to be understated, and with their artistry, their astounding technique, and their influence on African American musical styles to this day, they serve as excellent role models for twenty-first-century students of singing.

Popular Music: Rhythm and Blues to Rock and Roll
While in the case of bebop, Black musicians repudiated commercialism in the White music market and retained their artistic autonomy as creators and performers, the story of rock and roll is another inversion, in which the promise of enormous profit superseded the ethical responsibility of providing compensation for and artistic control over the music by its creators. The crux of the issue is described here, again, by Richard Crawford: "A key moment in American music history took place when teenagers' hunger for a music they could call their own combined with the popular music business's hunger for profits."[4] This is, of course, the origin of rock and roll, which is the story of how Black rhythm and blues came to be "packaged and marketed for White teenage audiences, chiefly by White performers,"[5] and can be pointed to as a clear example of appropriation. Whereas popular songs in the 1930s and 1940s were in the style of Tin Pan Alley with orchestral or big band instrumentation and polished vocals, rock and roll, like rhythm and blues, was guitar-based, and involved only a small group of players that undergirded a strong beat on drums and bass, fronted with raspy, shouted vocals. Great Black songwriters and performers of R&B were recording their music in the early 1950s, but their records stayed in the Black music market and on the R&B charts. However, because White musicians lived in close proximity to Black music in the South, they were well aware of those songs and their power, and essentially mined the gold of Black music for the White market. Songs that sold a few hundred thousand copies for Black artists became blockbuster hits for White artists, as in the case of Big Mama Thornton's 1953 recording of "Hound Dog," which was followed three years later by Elvis Presley's famous "top of the charts" recording of the same song.[6] Otis Blackwell's own recordings never made the top forty, but he wrote the songs that would soon propel Jerry Lee Lewis ("Great Balls of Fire") and Elvis ("Don't Be Cruel," "Return to Sender," "All Shook Up") to stardom, making him one of the unsung African American heroes of early rock and roll.

The case of rock and roll, however, represents an evolution to the pattern of appropriation and racialized commodification of Black vernacular music from earlier in the century; from its beginnings, rock and roll was consciously interracial. 1955 was the year that rock and roll first hit the "Top Fifty" charts of *Billboard* magazine, and the performers on that chart were both Black and White: Bill Haley and His Comets, Chuck Berry, and Little Richard. According to popular song historian Charles Hamm, "rock 'n' roll was thus established, in its first year, as an interracial music."[7] That year was to be a turning point in American culture not just because of popular music; Emmett Till was lynched in August of 1955, sparking a national awareness of White supremacist violence and the inhumanity of Jim Crow with its institutionalized racism, and the Montgomery bus boycott began in December of that year. In the following excerpt, music historian Richard Crawford again provides context for the intersection of popular song and societal change at this moment in history:

> Southern White youngsters were beginning to cross the color line to embrace so-called race music–at least as embodied in the new style called rock and roll. And that fact makes it seem no coincidence that in 1954-55, when the laws supporting segregation in the South were challenged, young White audiences around the country were embracing black-derived musical styles as their own. Teenagers who bought rock-and-roll records surely did so more as fans of the music than as champions of racial equality. Yet by accepting rock and roll with enthusiasm, White teenagers endorsed a sensibility shaped by Black Americans.[8]

That this sensibility was not shared by the older generation is well known. Fear of Black music and the social and racial integration it inspired created a strong White backlash that mirrored the resistance to dismantling Jim Crow in the South. But whereas popular music trends are often linked to transgressive disruption, the concert hall is an inherently conservative space, and has historically been very slow to react to the current moment. Changes to the status quo were then, as now, viewed with suspicion. Opera companies and symphony orchestras were seen as bastions of respectability, which meant that the changes in motion in American society would take much longer to breach the walls of classical music's conservative, Eurocentric power structure.

Concert Music: Barriers of Racism, Classicism, and Politics

From the late 1930s to the 1950s, classical music was still viewed by the scions of the Harlem Renaissance as the apex of aspiration for an African American composer. Though its widespread popularity was waning from its heights during the Gilded Age, and musical institutions were suffering from the effects of the Great Depression, concert music still held pride of place as a marker of cultural attainment. In the earlier era, Black composers were widely recognized for their achievements in concert music, largely as a list of "firsts" for the race. But during and after World War II, a combination of backlash conservatism and anti-communism rebounded on African Americans, making it difficult for them to express themselves artistically and politically. The House Un-American Activities Committee had enormous power to "blacklist" American artists suspected of being Communist sympathizers, and because of their activism for equality, many Black artists were targeted, such as bass-baritone Paul Robeson (1898–1976), who was blacklisted in 1950. Furthermore, it was still very difficult for African American actors and musicians to produce work that broke out of the mold of racist stereotypes. To orient our perspective, the movie *Gone with the Wind* was made in 1939, in which roles for Black actors were limited to stock slave caricatures for comic relief; amateur Blackface minstrel shows were being performed in communities all over the country; and actual Blackface minstrel performances by major stars were featured commonly and casually in Hollywood films (Fred Astaire, *Swingtime*, 1936; Judy Garland and Mickey Rooney, *Babes on Broadway*, 1941; Bing Crosby, *Holiday Inn*, 1942). So when an African American composer submitted a manuscript to a classical music publisher or attempted to have their symphonies or operas performed, chances are it was rejected for a variety of vague reasons, such as, it wouldn't sell because it doesn't sound either "classical" enough, or, on the other hand, "Black" enough, causing Black composers to confront an obstacle course of fungible criteria based on the whims of the White arbiters of access.

Take, for example, the case of William Grant Still's opera, *Troubled Island*. At first glance, it appears to be a success story for African Americans because it represents another compilation of "firsts": it was the first opera by an African American composer to be performed by a major opera company (New York City Opera, 1949), its librettist was the celebrated Harlem Renaissance poet Langston Hughes, and the cast featured a young baritone named Robert McFerrin (1921–2006) who would go on to be the first African American to win the Metropolitan Opera Auditions of the Air[9] in 1953. But if you dig deeper, the full story emerges of how the creators faced myriad hurdles to bringing the opera to life, and after only three performances, the opera itself wasn't produced again until 2009.

Although he was very well known as a symphonic composer in the 1930s, William Grant Still's favorite genre of composition was opera.[10] After a search for librettos that featured African Americans, Still approached

Langston Hughes, who offered his play *Emperor of Haiti* (about the Haitian Revolution in 1791) as a source, and they began work in 1936 to turn the poet's play into an opera. It was a rocky collaboration, made difficult by Langston Hughes' absence from the country to cover the Spanish Civil War, and personality differences that included Hughes' increasingly left-wing political engagement, whose opinions Still didn't share. After Hughes finally ended the partnership, leaving the finishing touches of the libretto incomplete, Still's wife Verna Arvey stepped in and provided the remaining text, and the work was completed in 1939. Still began to look for a major company to mount a production, and given his international stature as a composer he naturally turned to the Metropolitan Opera, who returned his score with an ambiguous explanation, as recounted by musicologist Tammy Kernodle:

> "In advising you that to our regret, we do not see our way clear to accept this work, we should like to point out that this conclusion should in no way be taken as implying any criticism as to the artistic merit of the work."[11] The rejection left the composer puzzled. After all, his symphonic works were performed all over the world, and his ballets had received repeated performances. Yet his hopes of having his opera produced were waning.[12]

The New York City Opera eventually expressed an interest in *Troubled Island*, but even with the backing and intervention of the legendary conductor Leopold Stokowski, who in 1945 described Still as "one of our greatest American composers,"[13] Still's opera was not produced there until 1949. The premier was received enthusiastically by the audience but much less so by the critics, who by turns described it as too "old school" operatic or, conversely, that it should be on Broadway rather than the opera stage. In 1950, even the recording met with mysterious suppression when it was abruptly pulled from European broadcast by the U.S. State Department, possibly due to Langston Hughes' leftist activism, for which he was called before the House Un-American Activities Committee in 1954.[14]

The Civil Rights Era and the Power of Black Song

As Black and White citizens came together in protest over the treatment of African Americans in the Southern United States, Black song became one of their most powerful tools for the expression of their ideals, solidarity, and determination. As early as 1939, when jazz great Billie Holiday first performed the now iconic anti-lynching song "Strange Fruit," with music and lyrics by the Russian Jewish immigrant Abel Meeropol, interracial collaboration was a vital component of the civil rights movement. Black musical genres in all styles were the soundtrack of this time, when "the singers transformed the repertoire of spirituals, gospel music, and rhythm and blues into freedom songs during sit-ins, marches, and freedom rides."[15] Spirituals, especially, proved to be adaptable to the purpose of protest, with new lyrics added to powerful songs such as "Oh Freedom," and "Ain't gonna let nobody turn us around," "but again and again they came back to 'We shall overcome,' making up hundreds of verses to fit the simple melody."[16] Popular music was at the forefront of protest as well, and artists made powerful statements with their songs, like Nina Simone's "Mississippi Goddam" from 1964. But Black activism wasn't limited to protest. In 1960, Berry Gordy founded the Motown Record Corporation, which became the first Black-owned record label to consistently produce crossover hits featuring Black artists, and "within a few years it had mushroomed into a huge conglomerate with a publishing arm, a management company, and recording studios, in addition to the record company."[17] Motown artists such as Smokey Robinson, Martha and the Vandellas, Diana Ross and the Supremes, the Jackson 5, and Stevie Wonder dominated the top one hundred charts for a decade, establishing a "unique 'Detroit Sound,' a music combining elements of rhythm 'n' blues, pop, gospel, and big band."[18] The pattern of White rock and roll artists appropriating the Black genre of R&B was thus inverted, with Black artists on the top one hundred reclaiming R&B for the civil rights era in the form of soul music, in which "soul singers voiced concerns about social injustice, racial pride, black militancy, and forms of protest; their music was correspondingly harsher, more intense, and more explosive than rhythm 'n' blues, with more emphasis upon traditional Black-music elements–such as gospel, for example–and performance practices."[19]

It is interesting to note, however, that despite the recognition and appreciation of Black music, there was still a White bias in American popular music, whether it was in the way the decade was reported (and thus remembered) or the way it was experienced by the still fairly segregated society at the time. For example, the famous music festival Woodstock was held for the first time in the summer of 1969 (August 15–18), with iconic performances by mostly White artists, from Janis Joplin to the Grateful Dead (although Jimi Hendrix's solo guitar rendition of the "Star-Spangled Banner" from Woodstock has had repercussions to this day).[20] But during the same period that summer (July–August), another music festival was held in Harlem that featured the African American giants of jazz, R&B, soul, pop, and gospel. It wasn't covered by television reporting even though it drew similar numbers of attendees, but who were, like all the performers, African American. The

"Summer of Soul," as filmmaker Questlove titled his 2021 movie featuring footage of these legendary performances, was dubbed "the most popular music festival you've probably never heard of,"[21] by *National Geographic*, but it's the subtitle of Questlove's film that completes the narrative. The full title, *Summer of Soul (. . . Or, When the Revolution Could Not Be Televised)*, reminds us that the lack of coverage for the Harlem Cultural Festival of 1969 was more than just an oversight; perhaps it was fear, or a purposeful attempt to silence Black voices in this era when popular music had done so much to disrupt the status quo.

Civil Rights and the Concert Hall

While Black musical genius was being increasingly recognized and remunerated in the world of popular music genres, Black music in the concert hall still faced persistent biases that served to exclude Black performers and composers. From *Brown v. Board of Education* in 1954 to the passage of the Civil Rights Act of 1964 (and beyond), Black classical artists faced a constant struggle with overt racism. In an anecdote related in *I Never Walked Alone*, legendary opera singer Shirley Verrett's autobiography, she describes an experience she had when Leopold Stokowski (the immensely powerful and influential conductor who was such a supporter of William Grant Still's) wanted to engage her to sing on a concert with the Houston Symphony Orchestra, where he was principal conductor. It was 1959, and she was on the cusp of a great career (she would become a winner of the Metropolitan Opera National Council Auditions in 1961, the same year as groundbreaking African American tenor George Shirley), but even the support of the most powerful conductor in the business was not enough to overcome racist opposition to her engagement from the symphony board. When Stokowski himself delivered the news that it would not be possible for him to hire her because he "was now an old man and tired of fighting," all she could say was,

> "Yes, maestro. I understand, maestro. Thank you, maestro. I appreciate your confidence in me, maestro." What else could I have done? What could most Black people do during that period? We could try to appear dignified and swallow our hurt and humiliation. I swallowed a lot, but not nearly as much as so many others had. I was in New York City and had lived in California, where things were only *slightly* better, or perhaps such feelings were covert. In the South, we suffered open racial insults and attacks. I was upset, almost to the point of crying, and then became angry about this kind of stupidity from supposedly cultured people.[22]

Verrett very soon established a career in which her extraordinary artistry was featured on all the top operatic and concert stages of the world, thereby having the last laugh on the "supposedly cultured people" of the Houston Symphony's board in 1959. Her autobiography was published in 2003, and like Questlove, Verrett made a special point with her choice of subtitle for her book: *The Autobiography of an **American** Singer* [emphasis added]. Her world-wide operatic fame granted her visibility and credibility, smoothing the way for subsequent generations of Black classical singers. Without a performer's visibility, however, African American classical composers struggled to make their voices heard.

The composer and pianist Margaret Bonds (1913–1972) was somewhat of a musical prodigy, composing her first piano piece at the age of five. She was from Chicago and grew up in a household surrounded by African American musical luminaries thanks to her mother, who was a charter member of the National Association of Negro Musicians. Estella Bonds generously fostered "musicians in need, and older Chicagoans recalled her Sunday afternoon musicales as one of the few places where aspiring young Black students could gather and meet famous African American creative artists: the singers Abbie Mitchell, Lillian Evanti, and Roland Hayes; the composers Will Marion Cook, William Dawson, and Noble Sissle; the poets Countee Cullen, Arna Bontemps, and Langston Hughes."[23] Florence Price was also a member of that community, and along with William Dawson, taught Bonds piano and composition before Bonds enrolled at Northwestern University in 1929, at the age of sixteen. By the time she received her Bachelor of Music (1933) and Master of Music (1934) degrees in piano and composition, Bonds had won a national Wanamaker prize for her art song "Sea Ghost," and performed with the Chicago Symphony Orchestra as a soloist, becoming the first African American to appear as a soloist with a major American symphony orchestra. One would think that such a high-achieving student would have been celebrated during her studies, but the attitude toward her at Northwestern was one of grudging tolerance rather than celebration. According to Helen Walker-Hill, author of *From Spirituals to Symphonies: African American Women Composers and Their Music*, Bonds was one of the few Black students there, where the atmosphere was hostile, racist, and nearly unbearable, and although she was permitted to study there, she was not allowed to live on campus.[24] She later moved to New York, where she supported herself playing for singers, musical theatre productions, and clubs, as well as continuously composing both popular and concert music. For a time she studied composition at Juilliard with Roy Harris, and worked at all the music jobs she could find, including being a choir director and performing as a piano duo with Frances Kraft Reckling. But through it all, composition was her consuming passion, and it was with her contributions to classic song that she "achieved her greatest depth and originality," in which she strove for a "marriage between words and music."[25] And it was through her song settings of Langston Hughes' poetry that Bonds established an African American voice for the concert hall in the civil rights era.

Bonds' friendship with Langston Hughes would be one of the central pillars of her life, personally and professionally. In the following excerpt from an interview by James Hatch, Bonds describes her first encounter with Hughes' poetry when she was a student at Northwestern University:

> I was in this prejudiced university, this terribly prejudiced place.... I was looking in the basement of the Evanston Public Library where they had the poetry. I came in contact with the wonderful poem, "The Negro Speaks of Rivers," and I'm sure it helped my feelings of security. Because in that poem he [Langston Hughes] tells how great the Black man is. And if I had any misgivings, which I would have to have—here you are in a setup where the restaurants won't serve you and you're going to college, you're sacrificing, trying to get through school–and I know that poem helped save me.[26]

(Incidentally, over thirty years later Northwestern University would honor her with their Alumni Merit Award, in 1967.) Bonds met Hughes when she was still in Chicago, in 1936, and they immediately began collaborating on songs (popular as well as classical), cantatas, and musical theatre projects. In her settings of "The Negro Speaks of Rivers" (1941) and *Three Dream Portraits* (1959), Bonds "employed the various musical languages she had mastered—traditional classical styles, jazz, and pop—in order to explore the complex inner lives of the poetic protagonists Hughes created."[27] With these songs, she brought the ideals of the Harlem Renaissance to a new cultural moment, and along with her masterful solo settings of Negro spirituals, sought to provide repertoire for concert performers that celebrated African American achievement. Bonds also "felt strongly about Black performers' obligation to include Black composers . . . on their programs when performing in White venues. 'God bless Betty [Allen] for taking us all out of the ghetto and not one of us will be completely out of it until *all American singers* [emphasis added] start thinking this way' (4 March 1966)."[28]

The 1970s and Beyond: Black Song in a "Colorblind" Culture

The protests and political turbulence of the civil rights era did not disappear overnight, but culturally, one could say that America emerged out of the wilderness of Jim Crow and entered a "Black Is Beautiful" phase. African and African American culture was celebrated with the Black Arts Movement starting in the mid-1960s; popular music captured the moment, as with James Brown and his 1968 song "Say it loud–I'm Black and I'm Proud," and Nina Simone's song from 1969, "Young, Gifted and Black"; the musical *Hair* appeared on Broadway in 1968 and *Purlie* in 1970; on television, *American Bandstand* was joined by *Soul Train* in 1971, and because of his hugely popular variety show on NBC, in 1972 *Time Magazine* dubbed Flip Wilson "TV's First Black Superstar."[29] A miniseries was made of Alex Haley's novel, *Roots: The Saga of an American Family*, and it was aired in 1977 on ABC. Its final episode ranks as number three on the list of the top-rated television shows of all time.[30] For a time, it seemed like White and Black America's interests were converging in a more inclusive way, leading to the ideal of a "colorblind" society.

It was during this period that bass-baritone Willis Patterson (b. 1930) became the first African American to join the faculty at the University of Michigan's School of Music, where he would have a lasting impact on students as well as the institution. Like Margaret Bonds, Patterson is a passionate advocate for the performance of concert music by Black composers, serving terms as president of the National Association of Negro Musicians as well as executive secretary of the National Black Music Caucus. In 1977, he published the first anthology of *Art Songs by Black American Composers*, in a logical but groundbreaking step to integrate the vocal music canon the same way television was exploring American identity through a Black lens with *Roots*. Knowing that resources by themselves were insufficient, he followed the publication of his anthology with the creation of a voice literature class dedicated to art songs and spiritual settings by African American composers. Yet his academic initiative did not produce widespread institutional change or result in the addition of art songs by Black composers into the concert repertoire included in voice performance curricula. And given the fact that classical music audiences are dwindling and musical institutions in the United States are perpetually underfunded, opera companies and symphony orchestras then (as now) have preserved their profits by assiduously avoiding rocking the boat. As a result of this economic and cultural conservatism, African American singers in the 1990s were still facing obstacles that, while not overtly racist, were certainly rooted in the Eurocentric power structure of classical music.

Ray M. Wade, Jr. was one of the many African American students that Dean Patterson recruited to the University of Michigan and mentored during his tenure. A native of Fort Worth, Texas, Wade was from a poor background

Figure 3.1. 1993 Met Competition Photo
Courtesy of the Met Competition.

Figure 3.2. Ray M. Wade, Jr.
Courtesy of Ray M. Wade, Jr.

but had an undeniable talent and a very strong desire to sing operatically. Incidentally, Wade said that when he arrived to begin studying with Dean Patterson, he had never sung spirituals outside of church, and certainly never art songs by African Americans, so Dean Patterson introduced him to the world of that repertoire as well as the standard European canon and made sure he sang it all with proper style and technically polished vocal production. Soon after Wade graduated he won the highest award a young artist can achieve in the United States; in 1993, he was one of the winners of the Metropolitan Opera National Council Award, which has jump started the careers of so many world-renowned American singers, such as Frederica Von Stade (1969), Thomas Hampson (1981), Deborah Voigt (1985), Stanford Olsen (1986), Renee Fleming (1988), and Susan Graham (1988).

Yet, after proving his worth at the highest level of attainment, Wade found himself unable to book an engagement in the United States. Again, he turned to his mentor for help, and Dean Patterson asked a friend to assist in setting up an audition for Wade at a German opera house; after one audition, he booked a contract with the National Theater Mannheim and has been living and singing professionally in Germany ever since.

The story of the beginning of Wade's career took place at a time in which the idea of a "colorblind" society held sway. But if opera were truly colorblind, then Ray M. Wade, Jr. would have been able to sing professionally in the United States. Not only was he a Met Competition winner, but he was a tenor, and good tenors are in notoriously short supply. Clearly, there were still barriers for African American men who were classical singers. On top of conservative casting conventions at opera companies who were still reluctant to present African American tenors as romantic leads, the barriers most likely began with childhood musical socialization; and if you were from an economically disadvantaged background like Wade, further barriers then and now include a lack of access to music education in public schools, lack of access to private piano lessons that form the foundation of classical musical training, and the prohibitive cost of higher education, which is a non-negotiable requirement for a classical singer in order to be prepared vocally, musically, and linguistically for a career. In 1996, Dean Patterson was likely frustrated with the lack of progress of his life's work when he felt the need to advocate for vocal concert repertoire by Black composers through the publication of an article that appeared in the *Black Music Research Journal*, entitled "The African-American Art Song: A Musical Means for Special Teaching and Learning." What follows are some passages from Patterson's article that are still profoundly relevant today:

It is clear that, given the sociological and academic difficulties of the times, we can ill afford to ignore any mechanisms that offer the potential to make valuable contributions to a more complete understanding of ourselves as Americans and of American history. African-American art songs represent an important contribution to that process—not only for the group from which they originate but also for all Americans.[31]

By contrast [to the canon of art songs of European composers], an impressive number of African-American art songs are based on texts that deal with the here and now, "nitty-gritty" circumstances of life and its travails. The lyrics of these art songs reflect the lives and conditions of such African-American literary figures as Paul Laurence Dunbar, Langston Hughes, Countee Cullen, Claude McKay, and Mari Evans. The musical forms to which these texts are set also tend to mirror the musical interests and circumstances of the artist's contemporaries. Consequently, one finds these art songs set in forms that arise from the blues, the jazz ballad, and gospel solo forms as well as those that are modeled after European song forms. All this lends a sense of currency to African-American art songs, rendering them much more accessible to contemporary performers and their audiences and heightening their effectiveness for teaching and learning. Much important information on the historical development of the African-American people during the late nineteenth and early twentieth century is contained in these songs. This information, which tends to be easily overlooked or forgotten in formal teaching situations, is vividly reflected in these texts and musical forms.[32]

He concludes his article with a prescient reminder of "the importance of the information contained in African-American art songs to that people and to that history. But, in truth, this information is of great consequence to all people—both within and outside the United States—who wish to gain a clear, comprehensive picture and understanding of American cultural and social history."[33]

The Twenty-First Century: Walk the Walk, Sing the Songs

Where do we go from here? Black song in all its forms has effectively documented every major epoch of our American history from slavery and the Civil War to reconstruction, segregation, and the civil rights movement. Blackface minstrelsy and its persistent racial stereotypes are hateful to us now, but by distancing themselves from the subjects, whether out of distaste, shame, or the desire not to cause offense, White Americans have nurtured a cultural amnesia and an unwillingness to confront how that legacy affects our society. That being said, we have a very powerful tool at our disposal to right this wrong. When singers of all races perform the songs of African Americans, we begin with our hearts, feeling the emotions that the music inspires, forming a bond of empathy. But then we must follow with our heads, studying and listening deeply to the words and music of these creators and learning about their historical contexts. And finally, we must take action. In the words of the Rev. Dr. Martin Luther King, Jr., set to music by composer Adolphus Hailstork (b. 1941) in his *Songs of Love and Justice* (1992), "Every man must decide. What are you doing for others? What are you doing?" As in the non-violent protests of the civil rights movement, we can use our bodies to perform the music, in a public demonstration of community, solidarity, and celebration.

Notes

1. Crawford, *America's Musical Life*, 756.
2. Crawford, *America's Musical Life*, 757.
3. Crawford, *America's Musical Life*, 767–68.
4. Crawford, *America's Musical Life*, 722.
5. Crawford, *America's Musical Life*, 722.
6. Hamm, *Yesterdays*, 408.
7. Hamm, *Yesterdays*, 394.
8. Crawford, *America's Musical Life*, 735.
9. The Metropolitan Opera Auditions of the Air was replaced by the Metropolitan Opera National Council Auditions in 1954.
10. Southern, *The Music of Black Americans*, 433.
11. William Grant Still, "Troubled History of *Troubled Island*," *New York Times*, March 20, 1949. The explanation for the rejection of *Troubled Island* was written by Edward Johnson, the general manager of the Met. Quoted in Tammy Kernodle, "Arias, Communists, and Conspiracies: The History of Still's *Troubled Island*," *The Musical Quarterly* 83, no. 4 (Winter 1999): 489.
12. Kernodle, "Arias, Communists, and Conspiracies," 489.
13. Southern, *The Music of Black Americans*, 431.
14. Kernodle, "Arias, Communists, and Conspiracies," 501.
15. Burnim and Maultsby, *African American Music*, 277.
16. Southern, *The Music of Black Americans*, 472. Southern goes on to say that "We shall overcome" was actually a pastiche of a spiritual (possibly "No more auction block for me") and a gospel song ("I'll overcome someday").
17. Southern, *The Music of Black Americans*, 515.
18. Southern, *The Music of Black Americans*, 515.
19. Southern, *The Music of Black Americans*, 517.
20. For an interesting discussion of the "Star-Spangled Banner" at the intersection of race and patriotism, see chapters 8 and 9 of Clague, Mark, *O Say Can You*

Hear? A Cultural Biography of the Star Spangled Banner (New York: W.W. Norton & Company, 2022).

21. Tucker C. Toole, "The most popular music festival you've probably never heard of," *National Geographic*, August 19, 2021, https://www.nationalgeographic.com/history/article/the-most-popular-music-festival-youve-probably-never-heard-of.

22. Shirley Verrett with Christopher Brooks, *I Never Walked Alone: The Autobiography of an American Singer* (Hoboken, NJ: John Wiley & Sons, 2003), 60–61.

23. Helen Walker-Hill, *From Spirituals to Symphonies: African American Women Composers and Their Music* (Westport, CT: Greenwood Press, 2002), 145.

24. Walker-Hill, *From Spirituals to Symphonies*, 147.

25. Walker-Hill, *From Spirituals to Symphonies*, 161.

26. Walker-Hill, *From Spirituals to Symphonies*, 156.

27. James Manheim, "Bonds, Margaret 1913–1972," *Contemporary Black Biography*, Encyclopedia.com, accessed December 20, 2022, https://www.encyclopedia.com/education/news-wires-white-papers-and-books/bonds-margaret-1913-1972.

28. Walker-Hill, *From Spirituals to Symphonies*, 156.

29. "Black is Beautiful: The Emergence of Black Culture and Identity in the 60s and 70s," Smithsonian National Museum of African American History and Culture, accessed January 4, 2023, https://nmaahc.si.edu/explore/stories/black-beautiful-emergence-black-culture-and-identity-60s-and-70s.

30. Bill Gorman, "TV by the Numbers: Top 100 Rated TV Shows of All Time," March 21, 2009, https://web.archive.org/web/20120919181719/http://tvbythenumbers.zap2it.com/2009/03/21/top-100-rated-tv-shows-of-all-time/14922/.

31. Willis Patterson, "The African-American Art Song: A Musical Means for Special Teaching and Learning," *Black Music Research Journal* 16, no. 2 (Autumn, 1996): 305.

32. Patterson, "The African-American Art Song," 305–06.

33. Patterson, "The African-American Art Song," 309.

SECTION II

INSTITUTIONAL INTERVENTIONS

CHAPTER FOUR

The Academy as an Agent of Restorative Justice through Pedagogy, Performance, Research, and Community Engagement

This chapter will explore how the music academy, an institution, or an individual (such as an independent teacher, teaching artist, professional and non-professional singer, or music consultant) can emerge as an advocate for restorative justice. In shedding light on the conscious underrepresentation of the Black voice in the canon, our goal is to tackle the issue of agency when offering a diversified selection of music traditions beyond our cultural identities. We can sustain respectful professional practices in teaching, performance, and research through conversations, community building, and trust. Whether working in educational institutions, community organizations, or private studios, each space faces unique challenges to developing a set of core values and establishing music ecosystems that include the local economy and cultural identities. However, we hope the ideas generated from this chapter can be useful for broad application to professional practice, curriculum reform, inclusive pedagogy, and community engagement.

Pedagogy

In theory, there are many pedagogical benefits that students and teachers will gain by exploring repertoire by Black composers, including cross-disciplinary connections that engage students in blended singing styles (classical and non-classical). Students may also develop more understanding and empathy for the Black experience in America and deepen their historical knowledge. Classical music instruction is often challenging for many students to embrace at first, but a spiritual or folk song arrangement can provide a pathway to engage students who may need more experience performing standard repertoire in the canon. This incremental approach will help develop the foundations of vocal technique that are required to successfully meet the complex demands of classical as well as non-European music idioms (i.e., off-beat melodic phrases, blues notes, slides [slurs], phonation through humming, polyrhythms, and poignant articulatory delivery).

We must also consider our approaches to teaching itself in order to create pedagogical frameworks that help shape a more inclusive curriculum. Perhaps an ideal situation would be to only enhance voice instruction by assigning BIPOC music, or to use the repertoire to provide cross-disciplinary connections and pedagogical benefits that engage students in singing across classical and non-classical vocal styles. However, students must go beyond learning the music to research and reflect on the context. What is our role as educators? Do we acknowledge that sustainable education takes place on both sides of the studio and classroom? Teaching is an interactive and responsive process; each partner (student and instructor) has unique work to do. Before the benefits of approaching, centering, and amplifying this repertoire can be realized, both students and teachers can begin by confronting barriers of ambivalence or hostility to the idea of performing repertoire by African American composers. To accomplish this task, it is helpful to bring to the forefront a variety of pedagogies to launch or re-fuel the work of bringing restorative justice to the canon of American song. A specific pedagogy or professional practice will guide teachers in a subject or idea for their students through a particular lens. In *Small Teaching: Everyday Lessons from the Science of Learning*, James Lang suggests that "the quickest method for cultivating retrieval practice in class takes the form of asking questions, either orally or in writing, about material that either you or the students have covered already."[1] Various pedagogies are now available to engage in transformative and intentional work on a race or culture-specific topic and beyond. A few foundational pedagogies in the following section are suggested to offer a framework to approach this purposeful work with context and respect (see figure 4.1).

Furthermore, creating inclusive and respectful learning spaces is imperative to thrive. For example, the Reinert Center for Transformative Teaching and Learning at Saint Louis University recommends "teaching methods to create equitable learning environments where all learners can be successful, regardless of the difference in identity, background, and ability. It involves an explicit commitment to recognizing and minimizing the potential for exclusion, from syllabus design to assessment methods, from instructional strategies to classroom layout."[2] Of course, any music instruction delivered either by independent or institutional teachers can subscribe to this model.

AFROCENTRIC:
This pedagogy is centered on African tradition across the diaspora and examines the preeminence of African and Black cultural traditions.

MULTIDISCIPLINARY:
As we work on a specific project or music event, multidisciplinary pedagogy allows us to call upon other fields as a lens to study further. For example, we could program a concert using the opportunity to connect to other colleagues in disciplines outside of our own to help students see the intersectionality of working on a specific topic.

CULTURALLY-RESPONSIVE:
Engaging in the study of responding to cultural influences and differences to guide our intentions, especially in teaching and the creative arts. One must always respect the cultural bearers and learn historical and political awareness to best prepare our students to forge meaningful connections through the arts.

EMPATHETIC:
In an article abstract on empathy in secondary education, Damianidou and Phtiaka (Department of Education, University of Cyprus) outlines a three-stage process during which a constant teacher-student interaction is present.

The first stage includes understanding the students' perspectives and giving value to their experiences. When the communication channels are open and teachers get into their students' shoes, material relevant to their experiences is presented in the second stage. In contrast, students are encouraged to question the prevailing status quo and raise their voices in institutional contexts where they have traditionally been silenced. Finally, during the third stage, students disseminate self-gained knowledge and thoughts to create a better future and a different society as part of the broader mission of informed, democratic, critical, empathetic, and active citizens (Damianidou and Phtiaka, 2016).

MINDFULNESS:
This involves thinking about other experiences and building upon areas of allyship. *Psychology Today* suggests that being mindful is "to objectively observe and label thoughts, feelings, and sensations in the body. Furthermore, mindfulness is a state of active awareness of the present moment without judging them as good or bad."

TRAUMA-INFORMED:
This is a timely one for several reasons at this given moment. Some historical subjects, such as slavery, lynching, racialized violence, minstrelsy, and discrimination, may involve ill feelings, discomfort, helplessness, shame, and guilt.

REFLECTIVE PRACTICE:
This involves the practice of continuous self-reflection to self-learning and to improve subsequent practices. Thus, this pedagogy engages us to find ways to connect and reflect on the learning experience alone.

CITATIONS
EMPATHETIC: Damianidou, Eleni and Helen Phtiaka. "A critical pedagogy of empathy: making a better world achievable." Pedagogies: An International Journal 11 (2016): 235 - 248.
MINDFULNESS:
psychologytoday.com/us/basics/mindfulness#:~:text=To%20be%20mindful%20is%20to,identifying%20and%20managing%20difficult%20emotions.
TRAUMA-INFORMED: oah.org/tah/issues/2015/may/trauma-and-trigger-warnings-in-the-history-classroom.
REFLECTIVE PRACTICE: Association of College and Research Libraries (ARCL) and American Library Association (ALA). "Five Things You Should Read About Reflective Practice, 2016. acrl.ala.org/IS/wp-content/uploads/5Things2016-1.pdf.

Figure 4.1. Pedagogical Framework
Stephens and Clark, 2023.

Performance

> The hallmark of African American art songs is that they serve as soulful expressions of the people's experiences. Projected through many of these musical expressions are important narratives on African Americans' emotional, cultural, and spiritual history (Willis Patterson).[3]

There remain concerns about equity and inclusion in higher education, specifically around the denegration of non-dominant identities, such as Black, Brown, Indigenous, and Asian voices, resulting in a lack of representation in the canon of classical music. However, performing artists of all ethnicities and across various genres have always been on the frontlines of social justice, so our music making and creativity can foster ways to build communities through activism as global citizens. As we approach community engagement through music and cultural competencies, all willing performers can and must honor cultural identities outside their own. If not, performances could be viewed as cultural appropriation when the intention of "why" the performer represents another culture's music is unclear or unaddressed.

As singers, we can contribute to the consciousness of America's diversity by centering inclusivity using the "lens" of music. This preparation must happen carefully and methodically during the research and study phase, and if more time is needed to seek out local artists and genre experts in the field, plan to move most respectfully and promptly toward concert planning and performance of works by composers of color. As artists, it is okay if we do not have all the answers, especially regarding diverse cultural identities, musical genres, nuanced ways of expression, and styles; but if we lack knowledge of the culture, we must ask for help since we cannot afford to skip this step in producing a contextualized experience. However, some creative ideas may emerge organically from planning concerts around certain themes, such as nationalistic composers, prominent and less prominent but impactful poets, and historical periods (i.e., Harlem Renaissance, post–World War). Alternatively, you can use the tactic of "bait and switch" with music, planning programs of repertoire you're familiar with and connecting it to something outside your "wheelhouse." For example, you could connect electronic music to traditional composition, jazz to opera, symphonic or chamber music of Black composers to hip hop, R&B, gospel, and spirituals (perhaps working backwards from the present to the past).

When attempting to expand the diverse voices in classical music, singers of all ethnicities must dedicate time and reflective practice to study and perform repertoire by Black composers. We must remember that education produces understanding—while dialogue fosters a sense of shared community—and intentional performance creates empathy and awareness of lived experiences. Following the birth of the Harlem Renaissance and the end of World War I, most trained musicians came from the Black church. In the book *What Do You Know about Blacks in Classical Music*, African American music (formerly referred to as Afro-American) fuses African and European musical elements and exhibits certain unique stylistic features, though it is primarily African in tone and conception.[4] The origin of European and American art songs was mainly secular, but with the emergence of classic concert arrangements of African American spirituals, there is also a spiritual counterpart. Many Black composers followed the example of Harry T. Burleigh (1866–1949), who played a pivotal role in developing American art songs. By the 1920s, Black singers had been classically trained and performed the concert spiritual alongside the standard European repertoire. While some see art songs as the music of the upper class, African American art songs achieved added significance from a different perspective by providing social and political commentary in music and elevating the stature of composers of African descent (see "Selected Song Anthologies and Collections").

Informed Research

Teachers of singing have structured literature courses dealing with art songs of American composers with no mention of Black composers and no knowledge of their song works or the various styles and techniques of their serious vocal writing (Willis Patterson).[5]

Engaging in personal or institutional research on a musical topic or program will yield a more compelling and competent performance experience, as Emery discovered in the summer of 2021, when he worked with two students over a ten-week period through the Collaborative Undergraduate Research & Inquiry program at St. Olaf College. They investigated the barriers to diversifying the canon and decentering Whiteness in concert music. The research study consisted of three distinct parts: an anonymous survey for educators and performers, focus groups of college-level music students, and interviews with experts in the field. Participants shared their experiences studying and performing music by composers of color more broadly and the barriers associated with the task. Even though we had limited time and a smaller sample size for the survey, we found that while intentional work is undoubtedly being done to amplify marginalized composers, the result is often decentralized and confined to individual choice rather than systemic change. Administrators and governing bodies may set an example for their students by programming, discussing, and integrating equal representation in the music curriculum. Usually, the trajectory has been, for many teachers, to teach what they have been taught. Moreover, they pass it down from generation to generation but rarely expand that reach to underrepresented voices outside of what they know. This cycle is one that the two student researchers and Emery worked to understand and disrupt through inquiry, by asking the following questions generated from focus group discussions, providing context for the critical themes that emerged in the summer of 2021:

1. Do you have experience performing music that reflects a cultural identity different from your own? If yes, elaborate. What sorts of experiences have you encountered?
2. Do you have access to resources that would allow you to find music by composers of color?
3. How do you approach your preparations when you perform music by composers of color?
4. How active is your school in programming and performing works by composers of color?
5. Has that activity changed in the last year? To what extent?
6. Describe your school's response to the summer of 2020 concerning the national conversation surrounding systemic racism. How did it affect the performing arts at your school?
7. What are the next steps?

We observed two main themes: 1) most of the work done in musical institutions to diversify the canon is student-driven, and 2) many students rely on their teachers when researching music by composers of color. In order to shift the traditional paradigm in music education toward a more equitable division of labor for this important work, we have grouped the responses and suggestions into categories for every member of your community's music ecosystem to consider:

- For teachers:
  - While some students rely on their professors to find music by composers of color, others mention that most of the resources they use are not available through their institutions.
  - A school can have many professors actively working for inclusion and a broader, more diverse canon, but if the efforts are not directed by the institution itself as well, students will perceive that the school is not doing enough.

- More than programming is needed. Refrain from expecting students to be satisfied just because the music of composers of color is programmed. Discuss why it is essential to do so and discuss new performance considerations. Make it an educational experience.
- For students:
  - Students can influence school policy more significantly than they expect. One student created an entirely new unit within their diction class because they wanted to include an unrepresented language. The professor needed to learn the language, so the student researched and created educational materials.
  - Everyone can benefit from learning more about performance practice and the history behind their musical selections.
- For institutions:
  - Even though new music is being purchased and added to institutions' music libraries, a great many scores still "are missing."
  - Academic music institutions have made a great effort to diversify the canon in the past year. Some institutions have allocated funds and changed the curriculum to fight for equity. Nonetheless, these are only the first stages of this fight, and there is still much to be done.
  - Schools need to program a diverse array of music within the subsection of composers of color, even if some elements are less connected to a specific cultural heritage.
- What applies to teachers, students, and institutions:
  - We will not reach equity until it is normalized for students and faculty to perform a full recital of songs written by a composer of color without calling the recital "special."
  - When performing music by a composer from a different cultural identity than your own, the piece should be performed with the same energy and excitement (including rehearsal time) as any other musical work.
  - Issues of representation exist on all sides—only a select number of composers get into important retreats, while publishers make choices based on whom they recognize from exclusive events. Teachers and performers only choose music that others have successfully programmed—all areas must make a conscious effort to be more inclusive.
  - A composer from a historically marginalized group does not mean their piece will be about that marginalization. Black composers do not only write spirituals.

Music preparation must go beyond the vocal technique, pitches, rhythms, and text to include an effort to embody the lived experiences and influences of the poet and composer who brought a song to life. While focusing on historical and cultural context and learning from the cultural bearers or experts in the field, we gain respectful permission to present music without hesitation or regret. Isn't it always satisfying to share your intention and research if someone asks why you chose to perform a specific song, song cycle, or concert?

Community Engagement

> My dream is that restorative justice, as a worldview inspired by indigenous insights and as a medium of holistic change—on intrapersonal, interpersonal, intragroup, intergroup, and systems levels—might help move us from an ethic of separation, domination, and extreme individualism to one of collaboration, partnership, and interrelatedness (Fanie E. Davis).[6]

Cultural competency, awareness, and community engagement through reflective practice will benefit audience members and performers. Bringing forth a respectful and informed performance from the practice room to the concert stage may require the preparation and use of many of the following educational resources for performers and audience members: program notes, pre- and post-concert talks, run-out performances, in-school visits, websites, podcasts, commissions, lecture-performances, artist interviews, articles, concert reviews, liner notes for recordings or virtual projects, and concert announcements. In programming diverse repertoire for concerts, music artists will offer an intentional reason to engage with anti-racism, diversity, equity, inclusion, and belonging for communities. Even in the twenty-first century, discussions on race in America and beyond are challenging and often met with emotional and physical resistance. Our shared humanity must be the touchstone for addressing topics that connect race to music, including systemic inequities, especially in crossover vocal training for twenty-first-century singers. In the article, "Singing African-American Spirituals: A Reflection on Racial Barriers in Classical Music," Lourin Plant adds that:

> A call to reflection on race at the start of the twenty-first century is easier said than done. America's history and racial legacy are strangely interconnected; together, they frequently overwhelm our best efforts to transcend their difficulties. Such enormity stymies our collective abilities to know how or where to begin—how to approach race issues that historically bind us together and, at the same time, polarize us.[7]

Education is an effective way to engage audiences. Many arts organizations invest resources to share messages about a concert season or special event. Often, teaching artists and lecturers are hired to curate programs as a way of building relationships with audiences and raising awareness of the themes that the programs will explore. In her presentation entitled "Exploring Racial and Gender Equity Beyond the Concert Hall" for the 2021 National Chamber Music America Conference, cellist and concert curator Sasha Ono, who is a member of the Chamber Music Collective, offered a list of questions for artists to consider before planning concerts:[8]

- What story are you trying to tell?
- What elements do you have to tell your story?
- Who is your audience, and what need are you fulfilling?
- Why is it personally important to you to start this project?
- What implicit biases do I have, and what privileges have I experienced in my life?
- What qualifies you specifically to tell that story?
- What do you want the audience to walk away with?
- What obstacles will you face in bringing this material to life?
- What are your fears about this specific project?

How can we be agents of restorative justice as musicians and serve humanity through the arts? Many artists enjoy curating new programs that consist of traditional repertoire, contemporary works, out-of-the-box collaborations, or new commissions. Do not hesitate to create innovative projects—make a brand and collaborate with others, including non-musicians who bring additional skills. Although a single artist's vision is often the impetus, local, regional, or national grants favor collaborations or the commissioning of music projects for groups, such as solo voice and piano, chamber, choral, or instrumental ensemble. What about a blended genre or interdisciplinary music composition (dance, spoken word, and music)? How about building partnerships with a community's business, health, and education organizations about diversity awareness or a social cause? Getting started is often the hardest part, but if you begin with conversations to find common ideas, building meaningful relationships with community partners will follow.

How do strategic programming and funding decisions merge? Research shows that organizations must develop a strategic plan, shared vision, and goals to serve a community effectively. Community-building is no small task and requires professional skills for individuals or organizations; but by taking the following actions, stakeholders can position themselves for success:

1. Develop clear strategies to accomplish goals, which may include writing mission and vision statements.
2. Establish regular meetings with a project team or artistic collaborators.
3. Choose a strategic focus on paper and social media.
4. Research the cultural history of a local community or region.
5. Find performance and social venues to build community capacity; invite business consultants or genre experts in programming initiatives.
6. Hire volunteers and staff for business purposes, such as fundraising, grant writers, website design, building a website, creating a newsletter, or concert program (with an advertisement page, for example).
7. Manage publicity and programming details, including radio announcements and physical and electronic mailings.
8. Hire musicians, sound engineers, lighting, or caterers.
9. Apply for arts grants (county, city, or state).
10. Coordinate bookkeeping, including tax preparation.
11. Examine best practices of similar models elsewhere.
12. Schedule regular pre-concert talks, interviews, or post-concert receptions with culture bearers, experts in the field, living composers, guest artists, and lyricists or poets.

Of course, each community project must be flexible and may present differently in each specific location; therefore, it is best to offer a starting point based on the community's needs and create and tailor an engagement strategy.

Notes

1. James Lang, *Small Teaching: Everyday Lessons from the Science of Learning* (Hoboken, NJ: Jossey-Bass, 2016), 29.
2. "Inclusive Teaching," St. Louis University, accessed January 13, 2023, https://www.slu.edu/cttl/resources/inclusive-teaching.php#:~:text=The%20Reinert%20Center%20considers%20inclusive,identity%2C%20background%2C%20and%20ability.
3. Patterson, "The African-American Art Song: A Musical Means for Special Teaching and Learning," 305.
4. Henry V.S. Thomas, *What Do You Know about Blacks in Classical Music* (Baltimore: Gateway Press, 1989), xi.
5. Willis Patterson, *Anthology of Art Songs by Black American Composers* (New York: E.B. Marks Music Corp., 1977), vii.
6. Fanie E. Davis, *The Little Book of Race and Restorative Justice: Black Lives, Healing, and U.S. Social Transformation* (New York: Good Books, 2019), 93.

7. Lourin Plant, "Singing African American Spirituals: A Reflection on Racial Barriers in Classical Vocal Music," *NATS Journal of Singing* 61, no. 5 (May/June 2005): 451.

8. Sasha Ono, "Exploring Racial & Gender Equity Beyond the Concert Hall," recorded at Chamber Music America's 2021 Virtual Conference, January 2021, video, 3:30, https://chambermusicamerica.org/?s=sasha+ono.

CHAPTER FIVE

∽

Influence and Inspiration
Understanding Context and Cultural Influences in Classical American Vocal Music

Teaching What We Know: How the Academy Assigns Value and Replicates Established Hierarchies

The canon has long been a sore spot for African Americans. Why is the canon so exclusively White, unapologetically excluding the musical works of Black composers? Who are the stakeholders or gatekeepers of the canon? Some teachers fear that adding more songs to the canon will cause the removal of other beloved repertoires. Is this true? Should we be required to think more broadly about the canon's present constitution? These are questions that music teachers from K–12 to post-secondary music faculty, departments, and institutions currently struggle to answer.

In this chapter, we acknowledge the current state of the canon of vocal music and how it was formed by centuries of Eurocentric and class-based assumptions. But since the purpose of this book is to envision a truly integrated, diverse, and representative body of American vocal music, we will tell the stories of the effects of being musically educated without accurate representation in the canon and follow by providing organic on-ramps for integrating songs by African American composers into our curricula and performances, using the familiar to access the unfamiliar in order to move beyond merely teaching what we were taught.

Culture and the Canon

The songs included in anthologies used by high school and college voice teachers have not changed much over the past several decades. As we have moved into the twenty-first century, attempts at change have often bumped up against some formidable obstacles presented by the way culture functions, often because those attempts were too isolated to make an impact, but few of us stop to think about how culture shapes almost every aspect of our lives. In an episode entitled "The French Knight's Guide to Corporate Culture" from the podcast, *Cautionary Tales*,[1] host Tim Harford gives a compelling list of the qualities of culture that are constantly at work in any society:

- Culture is a group phenomenon; it's something you share with other people.
- Culture is pervasive; it's all around you as water is around a fish.
- Culture is enduring; it doesn't change quickly.
- Culture is implicit; people say things and take actions without being able to articulate why.

The culture of the academy provides an excellent example of these forces at work. The broader American culture of classical music has consistently valued European (not to mention male) composers above those born here, even when we saw European composers taking inspiration from American sources, such as Dvořák pointing to Negro spirituals in his *New World Symphony* and Ravel's and Milhaud's compositions that were inspired by the revolutionary language of jazz. But since the late nineteenth century here in the United States, classism and racism have worked symbiotically to devalue African American voices in classical compositions, because of stereotypical notions of musical "Blackness," on the one hand still noxiously influenced by minstrelsy and racialized popular song, and on the other, rigid associations of Black music with popular genres. This act of conscious exclusion resulted in a near-total erasure of Black composers from the American classic song repertoire that has been unconsciously replicated in our academies for a century or more. In this respect, cultural time appears to function like geologic time, stretching across long periods of seeming stasis and dependability, only to disintegrate before our very eyes because of decay and violent disruption caused by tectonic societal shifts, such as a pandemic and the protests in response to the murder of George Floyd.

As an example of the impact of the pervasive and enduring exclusion of Black voices from the canon of American music, we provide the experiences of two extremely successful products of the academy. One is a highly regarded opera singer with a résumé that includes appearances at the Metropolitan Opera as well as a Grammy award, and who now teaches voice on the faculty of a state university; the other is a widely published musicologist whose area of expertise is American music, who was educated at top-ranked music schools.

Professor Myra Merritt is on the voice faculty of Bowling Green State University. She received her bachelor's degree from the Peabody Conservatory of Music and master's degree from the Catholic University of America and made her Metropolitan Opera debut in 1982.[2] Because of her impressive reputation and the fact that she is African American, we were surprised and not a little daunted when we saw that Professor Merritt wanted to take part as a *student* at the Singing Down the Barriers Institute in the summer of 2022. We reached out to her before our week of learning began to get a sense of her starting point and to let her know what we would be covering in our sessions, and she told us that she knew very little about the art song repertoire of African Americans and sincerely wanted to learn more. Emery and I asked ourselves, "How is this even possible?"—but of course, our own experiences in the academy should have provided the answer.

Professor Merritt's career as a singer mirrors that of many African Americans: she grew up singing spirituals, both in church and at home, where she spoke movingly of how her mother used to love singing spirituals around the house. But when she went to school, she left that behind to immerse herself in the world of classical singing and all the training and discipline that entails, which did not include any representation of the wide array of vocal repertoire by Black composers of classical music, including concert settings of spirituals. While studying at the prestigious Peabody Conservatory, she learned the vocal technique and the languages required to perform on the operatic and recital stages of the world, and, after her distinguished performance career, took a position teaching voice at a university where she could mentor the classical singers of the future. In her teaching career, she occasionally assigned concert spirituals only to her African American students, but never considered assigning them to her other students.

Over the course of the week we worked together at the summer institute, Professor Merritt grew very animated in our discussions and was extremely enthusiastic about all the new (albeit old) repertoire she was being introduced to. By the end of the week, she felt empowered to assign both art songs and spiritual settings by African American composers to all of her students, regardless of their ethnic backgrounds. The important pieces of the puzzle that fell into place for her were, first and foremost, lots of new repertoire to explore (i.e., information allowing her to begin completing the canon), but a close second was permission (i.e., justification as well as strategies for having conversations with her students around the importance of performing this repertoire). Recognizing that she could make a difference beyond just her studio teaching, Professor Merritt also made arrangements to bring an expert to her campus (Dr. Louise Toppin from the University of Michigan School of Music, Theatre & Dance) to work with all the voice students at Bowling Green State University in order to lay this neglected foundation for the entire department and, hopefully, for the institution as well.

Professor Mark Clague is an associate dean and tenured professor of musicology at the University of Michigan School of Music, Theatre & Dance, from which he also received his undergraduate degree. Clague went on to receive his MA and PhD in musicology from the University of Chicago. For many years, both schools have consistently been ranked at the top of the list of excellent music schools in terms of both scholarship and performance, but during Professor Clague's time as a student in musicology, the music of African Americans was not given serious attention in the curriculum at the undergraduate or graduate levels. In this respect, the institutions were by no means outliers; it was most certainly the case at other peer, predominantly White institutions. It is striking, however, that this omission, in the case of the University of Michigan, not only coexisted with but was unaffected by the pioneering contributions of Dean Willis Patterson's scholarship and teaching of vocal repertoire by African Americans in the voice department at that time.

In his professional career, Professor Clague (a White musicologist) has been a tireless advocate for studying all strands of American music and its intersection with culture, with a significant emphasis on Black composers, creators, and performers.[3] But the story behind his impressive body of publications begins with a realization that came after he had earned his doctorate and taken a position at the Center for Black Music Research (CBMR) at Columbia College in Chicago, Illinois. There, working with musicologist Dr. Samuel Floyd, he received a supplemental yet foundational education that would significantly affect the trajectory of his scholarly career. Here is how Professor Clague describes his discovery of what he hadn't learned in school:

> My realization that I had failed to learn enough about Black musicians came when I arrived on the job at CBMR as an editorial assistant on the *International Dictionary of Black Composers* and saw a list of several thousand composers of which I only knew a handful = William Grant Still, Florence Price, Duke Ellington, and Louis Armstrong. The other formative experience for me was running the chamber music program of the Chicago Youth Symphony and organizing an annual Music of the Harlem Renaissance performance. Through that performance I came to know the music of George Walker, Samuel Coleridge-Taylor, and Joseph Boulogne.[4]

Individuals are not to blame for the omission of Black composers from our curricula, but its effect on individuals is undeniable. As a result of generations of replicated exclusion from the academic canon of American classical composers, the case studies of Professors Merritt and Clague demonstrate that a dedicated individual must go to extraordinary lengths to learn more about and advocate for this repertoire. But despite the fact that it takes exceptional perseverance for single individuals to overcome the forces of culture, these remarkable educators provide hope that there are many more like-minded faculty and administrators in the academy who, with better access to information and effective tools for communication, could re-examine the canon from a more inclusive perspective and marshal institutional forces in such a way as to make a significant impact on its culture.

Entry Points for Centering Black Composers of Classic Song and Opera: Acknowledging the Academy as a Historically White Space

Imagine a party. If you're the host, you control the guest list; if you are invited, you make the decision to attend because you want to socialize with old friends or meet interesting new people. Sometimes we know most of the other guests at the party, sometimes we don't, and we depend on the person who invited us to introduce us and make us feel welcome. In the following section, we consider how it feels to be invited to parties in different spaces represented by the music we choose to perform and teach, because a recital program is like a curated gathering of many different, incredibly interesting people: poets, composers, performers, and everyone in the audience.

We begin with the status quo. Figure 5.1 represents essentially two parallel parties that have been going on for over a hundred years, and provides examples of Black composers that have contributed to American art song repertoire alongside their White counterparts, who are the ones represented in the standard anthologies and library collections (see figure 5.1).

These juxtaposed lists demonstrate how the concept of Black "double consciousness" (a term coined by W.E.B. Du Bois in 1903) coexists with what we could call the "half consciousness" of the dominant, White culture of the academy. Since the academy has been officially desegregated for a while now, we think it's high time the academy expanded its guest list and invited all those who share the academy's culture and interests to the party. In the following section, using the familiar as a bridge to the unfamiliar, we present four song comparisons as examples of possible entry points for Black

REPRESENTATIVE AFRICAN AMERICAN COMPOSERS	REPRESENTATIVE WHITE COMPOSERS
H.T. Burleigh (1866–1949)	Amy Beach (1867–1944)
J. Rosamond Johnson (1873–1954)	Charles Ives (1874–1954)
Florence Price (1887–1953)	John Alden Carpenter (1876–1951)
Hall Johnson (1888–1970)	Charles Griffes (1884–1920)
William Grant Still (1895–1978)	Douglas Moore (1893–1969)
Undine Smith Moore (1904–1989)	John Duke (1899–1984)
Howard Swanson (1907–1978)	Aaron Copland (1900–1990)
Mark Fax (1911–1974)	Samuel Barber (1910–1981)
Margaret Bonds (1913–1972)	Gian Carlo Menotti (1911–2007)
Robert Owens (1925–2017)	Ned Rorem (b. 1923)
Betty Jackson King (1928–1994)	Lee Hoiby (1926–2011)
David Baker (1931–2016)	Dominick Argento (1927–2019)
Leslie Adams (b. 1932)	Libby Larsen (b. 1950)
Charles Brown (1940–2021)	John Musto (b. 1954)
Adolphus Hailstork (b. 1941)	Lori Laitman (b. 1955)
Anthony Davis (b. 1951)	Tom Cipullo (b. 1956)
Regina Baiocchi (b. 1956)	Ricky Ian Gordon (b. 1956)

Figure 5.1. Representative African American Composers and White Composers
Stephens, Helton; Clark, 2023.

composers into the White space of canonical recital repertoire, beginning with Amy Beach's invitation to her younger contemporary, Florence Price.

Song Case Studies

Getting to Know You: Amy Beach and Florence Price

Amy Beach and Florence Price had a lot in common. They were both concert pianists and pioneering women symphonic composers: Amy Beach was the first woman composer to publish a symphony (premiered by the Boston Symphony in 1896), while Florence Price was the first African American woman composer to have a symphony performed by a major orchestra (premiered by the Chicago Symphony Orchestra in 1933). They also both made major contributions to the repertoire of American classic song, but due to the dual barriers to publication of gender and race, Price's songs have been much harder to find than Beach's, which now appear in standard American song anthologies. The good news is that this disparity is being rectified, most recently with many new recordings of Price's works, and by the publication in 2015 of a volume dedicated to her songs.[5] However, since it takes a bit of effort to welcome a new guest to the recital program, please allow us to make an introduction in the spirit of discovering what the composers have in common by comparing two of their songs: "Ah, Love, But a Day!" by Beach and "Sympathy" by Price.

Amy Beach published her most famous set of songs (*Three Browning Songs*, Op. 44), set to poetry by Robert Browning, in 1900. "Ah Love, But a Day" is the second song, and it takes a through-composed dramatic journey in forty-eight measures that requires a high level of musicianship and skill on the parts of both singer and pianist. Written in late-Romantic harmonic language, it is chromatic and modulatory and quite passionate, with an operatic approach to vocal writing that befits the emotional struggle of the poet, who speaks in first person. The tessitura is high in the voice and the melody demands full expressive control from *pp* to *ff* from the singer. In the high key (f minor-f major), the voice ranges from Eb4 to A5, which is supported by a piano accompaniment that increases in intensity, texture, and virtuosity over the course of the song to the climax in m. 40. This song is very popular with fuller-voiced sopranos who are comfortable with their high ranges. If these same sopranos were looking for other repertoire to showcase their strengths, they would do well to perform "Sympathy" by Florence Price. Set to the famous poem by Paul Laurence Dunbar (The first line is "I know what the caged bird feels, alas!"), its dramatic journey takes place in fifty measures of vocal and pianistic virtuosity and late-Romantic chromaticism, but this journey is a bit more intense. In the (high) key of G major, the vocal range encompasses D4 to B5, and the generally high tessitura demands a similar level of expressive control from the singer at the top of the staff to the Beach. Also with a text in first person, its structure is ABA,[1] with a straightforward diatonic melody and regular phrasing in the A section that represent a cage of propriety, but in the B section you hear a violent struggle to challenge the harsh restrictions of the metaphorical cage through Price's chromatic harmonies, irregular phrase lengths, chromatic and disjunct melody, and rhythmic accents. The A section returns when the singer has spent her rage and appears to be reconciled to the status quo, but in a last assertion of dignity, the final phrase ascends to a sustained B5 marked with a fermata on the words "I know," and the remaining words of the sentence, "why the caged bird sings," are all set above the staff in an act of vocal defiance. It is a thrilling and passionate song for the performers and the audience alike, and we wager that Amy Beach would have loved it.

Influence and Inspiration: The Beauty of Shared Culture
The opening of this chapter focused on the deleterious effects of culturally enforced ignorance, but there is also a bright side to sharing culture. When human beings live in one society, it is inevitable that many of those human beings, regardless of their ethnic backgrounds or social status, will develop a shared admiration for its foundational works of art, music, and literature, and that mutual influence is particularly evident in American song. We chose to compare the following songs because each takes its text from a monumental poet of the English language: William Shakespeare and Langston Hughes. Most Americans are well aware of Shakespeare's vaunted place in the canon, and many are of Langston Hughes' impact as well, seeing that he is the most well-known and revered of the Harlem Renaissance poets, so it is only natural that all American composers would be drawn to set their poetry. The first song of our comparison is by Betty Jackson King (1928–1994), a Black American pianist, singer, educator, choral conductor, and composer,[6] who, in 1976, set the poem "In the Springtime," by Shakespeare; the second is by John Musto (b. 1954), a White American composer and pianist[7] who wrote a set of songs in 1986 called *Shadow of the Blues* to poetry by Langston Hughes, from which "Litany" is taken. Musto called it "Litany," but Hughes' title was "Prayer (2)." Because both are slow, in a medium range that only encompasses an octave, and very accessible musically, they are ideal for a young singer working on phrasing and expression without the challenges of virtuosic vocalism. King's setting, in keeping with the simple, familiar Shakespeare text ("In the springtime, the only pretty ringtime"), gives us a tender, strophic song in 3/4 with a lyrical and diatonic melody accompanied in the piano part by flowing arpeggiated figures in the left hand and chords

that often double the melody in the right. While King's setting is metrically regular, Musto's setting of Hughes' heart-wrenching prayer unfolds in a timeless feel of fluctuating meters at a slow tempo with text delivered in an emotion-based declamation, sometimes stretching syllables out, sometimes in short fragments, sometimes in lyrically expansive sentences. The harmonies in the piano part are filled with poignant suspensions, and over this constant wash of sonic suffering he gives space for maximum emphasis on the sound and meaning of the words by keeping the piano part separate from the vocal line, with text often being declaimed over long-held chords after an invitation by the piano on most down beats, sounding like a sorrowful call and response. Both of these songs have long, atmospheric piano introductions and demand the utmost sincerity on the part of the singer in their presentation and vocal delivery. Each of these composers has distilled the essence of the texts into moving musical expression with their unique compositional approaches and reverence for great English-language poetry, and both songs could serve as the beginnings of a recital program that features shared culture by showcasing songs by composers and poets of different ethnic backgrounds.

The Special Case of Black Opera in Academic Concert Settings

While recital repertoire is mostly drawn from the canon of classic song, opera arias are very often on the program as well. Performing an aria with piano in a recital setting is excellent training for a young singer as a first experience with that vocally challenging genre, helping the singer to get a sense for the boundaries of their instrument and exploring their *Fach*,[8] all while portraying a specific character with emotional and dramatic depth. These recital arias often form the foundation of a young artist's "package," a group of arias which they will use for countless auditions as they progress in their education and performance opportunities. The calculations that go into choosing "just the right arias" leave little room for experimentation, and, for practical purposes, students and teachers are often loath to break new ground with a choice that might seem too far out of the box. These practical considerations, combined with how hard it is to find excerpted arias from operas by Black composers, not to mention the ambivalence about portraying a character in a Black story, present some very daunting barriers to integrating the operatic canon. But since Black American opera[9] has been around just as long as White American opera, it makes sense to explore the realities behind its obscurity and imagine ways to weave it into the repertory of opera companies and recital programs. The following aria comparisons try to accomplish both of those tasks.

Rich Man, Poor Man

The composers Douglas Moore (1893–1969) and Mark Fax (1911–1974) were roughly contemporaneous and were both organists and pianists. Whereas Mark Fax was a child prodigy and was playing organ for silent movies in theaters by the time he was fourteen, Douglas Moore didn't start creating music until he was in college at Yale University, where his talent for writing popular tunes caught the attention of the music department chair, who persuaded Moore to pursue a second degree in music composition. Fax began his composition studies at Syracuse University but transferred to Eastman to study with the influential composition teacher Howard Hanson, and while there, he was awarded a Julius Rosenwald Fellowship, a fund established for the purpose of supporting the creative and academic ambitions of Black intellectuals. On the surface, it appears that both of these young composers were off to a propitious start at excellent universities, but their professional paths then diverged as a direct result of their disparate social and economic classes.

After graduation, Moore followed the familiar path of most American composers in the early twentieth century. He studied composition in Europe with Vincent D'Indy and Ernst Bloch, and even with Nadia Boulanger for a time. This period of post-graduate European study was made possible by the fact that Moore's father was very wealthy and left his son well provided for after his death in 1915. After his return from Europe, Moore took a position on the composition faculty of Barnard College at Columbia University and stayed there for nearly four decades, with regular residencies at the MacDowell Colony, where he composed many of his major works, including the opera *Giants of the Earth*, which won the Pulitzer Prize for music in 1951. Incidentally, Moore dedicated his first symphony (*A Symphony of Autumn*) to Fax's composition teacher, Howard Hanson, who conducted its premiere in 1931.[10]

Contrast the story of Douglas Moore's career with that of Mark Fax. First of all, there is a wealth of information about Moore available on the internet, but when you google Fax or even search the *New Grove Dictionary*, you're lucky to find more than a paragraph. What we do know is that, during the Depression, and after Fax was awarded the first of his two Julius Rosenwald Fellowships, he had to discontinue his studies and take a job at an HBCU in Georgia in order to support his family. In 1942, Fax returned to Eastman to continue his studies, but out of financial necessity took a job at a church in Rochester as choirmaster *and* janitor. It was during this period that he was awarded a rare second Julius Rosenwald Fellowship. In 1947, Fax joined the faculty of Howard University, a renowned research university and HBCU in Washington, DC, where he taught music theory and composition, also serving later on as director of the School of

Music and then acting dean of the School of Fine Arts, retiring after twenty-five years of service.[11]

Douglas Moore's opera, *The Ballad of Baby Doe*, premiered in 1956 and is the only one of his several operas that continues to be performed. Its tuneful music and its libretto based on a true story of the Gilded Age and westward expansion reflect back to opera audiences their expectations of American history, riches, rags, and individualism. Baby Doe's character is written for a light coloratura soprano, and her first aria, "The Willow Song," is a standard part of any young high soprano's audition package. Its folk-like melody, simple ABCA structure, and regular phrase lengths show the beauty of the voice and provide opportunities for floaty high notes and legato phrasing that epitomize Baby Doe's innocence and youth. The key is B-flat major, the meter is a dreamy 3/4, and the range is F4 to D6; it is forty-six measures long (not counting the introduction) and ends with a sustained F5 for two measures. This aria appears in the standard opera anthologies used by voice students throughout the country.

Mark Fax's opera, *A Christmas Miracle*, premiered in 1958, according to newspaper accounts, but no score is available to the public, and there is no other record of its being performed since then. A single aria from the opera, "Cassandra's Lullaby," is only available in Willis Patterson's *Anthology of Art Songs by Black American Composers*, but once you find it, it's clear the aria serves a dramatic role very similar to "The Willow Song" and is composed for the same voice type (a high, light soprano) and features the same regular phrase lengths and floaty, legato singing. Its form is also ABCA, in the key of A minor and a suitably slow and rocking 4/4 meter. Although the range is not as wide, from E4 to A5, the tessitura is very similar, hovering at the top of the staff, and at thirty-six measures, it has a similar length. "Cassandra's Lullaby" ends with a sustained A5 for two measures.

Two American operas premiered within two years of each other. There are good reasons why *The Ballad of Baby Doe* entered the repertoire of opera houses and recital stages, but wouldn't you like to at least be able to hear Mark Fax's opera and make a comparison? Mark Fax's opera couldn't pass through the barriers created by Jim Crow in the opera house and the publishing companies in 1958, so we'll never know. But this one aria we have is hauntingly beautiful and leaves us a clue to what we're missing: a gem of American opera.

A Tale of Two Bobs

Every undergraduate voice teacher with young baritones is likely familiar with "When the air sings of summer" (otherwise known as "Bob's Bedroom Aria") from *The Old Maid and the Thief* by Gian Carlo Menotti (1911–2007). Like "The Willow Song," this aria appears in standard anthologies and is regularly represented on recital programs and at opera auditions. But there is another baritone named Bob in the opera *Highway 1, USA* by William Grant Still (1895–1978), and his aria provides an excellent opportunity for a student with that voice type to explore a contrasting musical style and approach to dramatic characterization.

William Grant Still's importance as an African American composer of classical music cannot be overstated. His biography is a list of firsts: the first African American composer to have a complete score performed by a leading symphony orchestra (his first symphony, the *Afro-American Symphony*, conducted, incidentally, by Howard Hanson), which was from 1931 to 1950 the most performed symphonic work by any American composer; the first to have an opera performed by a major opera company (*Troubled Island*, New York City Opera, 1949, discussed in chapter 3) and to have one performed on television (*A Bayou Legend*, 1981); and the first African American to conduct a major symphony orchestra. He began his career playing in pit orchestras in New York and for Black companies on tour as well as arranging and orchestrating the music of others, but then moved on to composing for film, television, and the concert hall. His output includes nine operas, five symphonies, four ballets, as well as art songs, choral music, and chamber music. Still's one-act opera, *Highway 1, USA*, was composed over a period of years in the 1940s but didn't receive a premiere until 1963.[12]

Gian Carlo Menotti, although he was Italian, is primarily known as an American opera composer. His twenty-five operas comprise almost his entire output, and all of them are in English with libretti he wrote himself. He began his conservatory studies in Italy at the age of thirteen, but at seventeen traveled to the United States and began studying at the Curtis Institute of Music in Philadelphia, and he spent the rest of his life as a resident of the United States with his partner, composer Samuel Barber. He rejected the compositional influence of atonality that was prevalent in the first half of the twentieth century, opting instead for his own brand of Italianate lyricism inspired by Puccini and Mascagni, and many of his operas are produced in college programs because of their generally intimate, chamber-like dimensions. Interestingly, his opera *The Old Maid and the Thief* was written for radio on a commission from NBC and premiered on a broadcast in 1939.[13]

The character of Bob in *The Old Maid and the Thief* is a sort of handsome *tabula rasa* onto which Miss Todd and her housemaid Laetitia project their desires, providing the ironic dramatic twists which drive the story. Bob sings this aria when all the machinations in the household get to be too much for him and he decides it's time to move on, being the wanderer that he is. In keeping with Bob's vapid nature, the aria unfolds in a passive, wandering way, with a syllabic text setting and mostly stepwise melody at an andante tempo. He can't even muster the discipline to stay in one meter, just wandering from one phrase to the next in a declamation-based series of shifting meters from 4/4 to 5/4 and back again. Even the key wanders, but not in a Straussian energetic exploration; it feels more like Bob is visiting pictures in a museum, passing from experience to experience, starting the aria in F major and ending up at D minor/major. There is one moment of revelatory self-knowledge, in which he exclaims in a phrase that begins with the highest note in the aria ("Ah! The sharp joy of freedom"), which is also the one moment of harmonic dissonance and metrical expansion and contraction (6/4 to 3/4). With a range of A2 to F4 and a middle voice tessitura, it is an excellent aria for a young baritone to study vocally, but not a very compelling dramatic exercise.

Highway 1, USA is the story of a hardworking husband and wife who own and run a gas station and lead decent, upstanding lives on their modest income, surrounded by a community of working-class friends and neighbors. The husband, our Bob, has a younger brother, Nate, whose intelligence destined him for more than a life of manual labor, so Bob promised their mother on her deathbed that he would fulfill her dream of Nate's going to college. Bob and his wife, Mary, saved and sacrificed to provide for his education, but after Nate graduates, instead of fulfilling the high hopes of his family, returns to live off of Bob and Mary, giving them nothing in return but his scorn and derision for their working-class mentality and existence. This Bob's aria is called "A Dream Wasted," and in it, Bob realizes that Nate will never get a job, much less fulfill his intellectual promise, and that he has wasted years in the service of his ungrateful brother. In the first section of the aria Bob grapples with that realization, and in the chromatic and foreboding middle section, he expresses his anger and contempt for Nate's laziness and condescension. But in the final section, he remembers their dear, departed mother and how wise she was, and because she loved and believed in Nate, he resolves to try again to find the good in his brother.

Still's musical style here is very dramatic, which is well suited to this moment of crisis in Bob's life. The text setting is syllabic, and the phrases unfold in thoughts of varying lengths, allowing for a more realistic delivery of his tempestuous feelings. The range is D3 to F4 and sits in the higher part of the lyric baritone range, with stepwise melodic gestures that often rise to D4, Eb4, or E4 and then fall off. This Bob's highest note is also F4, and it comes at an emotional high point when he is talking about his mother in the last section of the aria.

Highway 1, USA and *The Old Maid and the Thief* were written around the same time, and both have a very Depression-era feel. None of the characters are from high society—all of them are struggling to make ends meet. Neither is set in an exotic locale, and both plots are driven by everyday characters, with their challenges and relationships. Each aria dramatizes a very different kind of person with different needs and goals but are both suitable to the same singer. The score of *Highway 1, USA* is available from the William Grant Still Music website,[14] but not in anthologies. Why not put the two Bobs in conversation on a recital program?

Notes

1. Tim Harford, "The French Knight's Guide to Corporate Culture," *Cautionary Tales*, June 17, 2022, https://timharford.com/2022/06/cautionary-tales-the-french-knights-guide-to-corporate-culture/.

2. For more information about her career, please visit her Bowling Green State University faculty biography: https://www.bgsu.edu/musical-arts/faculty-and-staff/myra-merritt.html.

3. For more information about his scholarly contributions, please visit his University of Michigan faculty biography: https://smtd.umich.edu/about/faculty-profiles/mark-clague/.

4. Mark Clague, email to author, December 15, 2022.

5. *44 Art Songs and Spirituals by Florence Price*, edited by Richard Heard and available from Classical Vocal Reprints, https://www.classicalvocalrep.com/products/44-Art-Songs-and-Spirituals-by-Florence-B-Price-for-Medium-High-Voice-and-Piano-Richard-Heard-205398.html.

6. "Betty Jackson King," African Diaspora Music Project, accessed September 23, 2022, https://africandiasporamusicproject.org/node/3208.

7. See John Musto's website: http://www.johnmusto.com/.

8. *Fach* is a German term used to refer to classical voice type classifications (i.e., lyric soprano, dramatic mezzo soprano, etc.).

9. See Naomi André's groundbreaking book, *Black Opera: History, Power, Engagement* (Urbana, IL: University of Illinois Press, 2018).

10. Andrew Stiller, "Moore, Douglas S(tuart)," *Grove Music Online*, 2001, https://doi-org.proxy.lib.umich.edu/10.1093/gmo/9781561592630.article.19063.

11. Velma Jones, *The Life and Works of Mark Oakland Fax* (Thesis); cited in "Mark Fax," *The African Diaspora Music Project*, accessed September 23, 2022, https://africandiasporamusicproject.org/mark_fax; https://en.wikipedia.org/wiki/Mark_Fax.

12. Gayle Murchison and Catherine Parsons Smith, "Still, William Grant," *Grove Music Online*, 2001, https://doi-org.proxy.lib.umich.edu/10.1093/gmo/9781561592630.article.26776.

13. Bruce Archibald and Jennifer Barnes, "Menotti, Gian Carlo," *Grove Music Online*, 2001, https://doi-org.proxy.lib.umich.edu/10.1093/gmo/9781561592630.article.18410.

14. http://www.williamgrantstillmusic.com/WorksforStage.htm; http://www.williamgrantstill.com/AriasDuetsandScenes.htm.

CHAPTER SIX

Centering the African American Experience

Spirituals and Non-Classical Genres in the Voice Studio

"The true history of blacks is not to be found in the history books, but in our music."

–Quincy Jones

Spirituals as Common Ground: Creating a Pathway to Learning History through a Black Lens

In this moment of the twenty-first century's reckoning with racial equality, anti-racism, inclusion, and belonging that stems from decades of exclusion and erasure, we are interested in exploring the pedagogical potential of learning our shared history through listening to African American creative voices, beginning with spirituals. Even though spirituals originated as folk songs unfettered by Western music notation and imbued with West African cultural traditions, these songs continue to resonate as spaces that provide historical context and a connection to the ancestral cultural bearers who created this music in America. We are still programming and singing these religious folk melodies; however, the songs we perform today are newly composed arrangements that were created after Emancipation. Zora Neale Huston has labeled all the concert performances of spirituals from the Fisk Jubilee Singers and other college ensembles as "neo-spirituals," and these religious folk songs now constitute a large genre of concert singing for solo voice and choral ensembles. Regarding historical accuracy, Hurston argues that "there never has been a presentation of genuine Negro spirituals to any audience anywhere. What is being sung by the concert artists and glee clubs are the works of Negro composers or adaptors based on the spirituals. Under this head come the works of Harry T. Burleigh, Rosamond Johnson, Lawrence Brown, Nathaniel Dett, Hall Johnson, and [John Wesley] Work."[1]

The fact that the spiritual arrangements we know and love are not, in Hurston's words, "genuine," actually misses the point. In centering African American culture through the study, preservation, and performance of concert spirituals, we can acknowledge this indigenous genre, passed down through the generations, as a foundational source for American song in both classical and contemporary commercial music genres. Spirituals originated from a dark past in American history, but they bring forth a legacy of hope, resilience, faith, and strength to generations removed from the era of slavery in the United States. Just imagine if every student had the opportunity to sing one or more concert spirituals for voice and piano. How would that influence teaching a more inclusive pedagogy of American music beyond the traditional canon? In the following chapter, we seek to provide the reader with some on-ramps for the respectful conversations necessary to educate and inspire performers and audiences when confronting the shared histories of this genre.

Entering the Black Space of the Concert Spiritual with Cultural Humility and Knowledge

Upon hearing a concert spiritual, the music and its legacy engage listeners in an unforgettable experience. As we approach the performance of concert spirituals, we must prepare ourselves for that task by using the many resources available on their respectful performance practice informed by cultural relevancy.[2] In Cheryl Sushell Bibbs' book, *The Art of the Spiritual: Enhancing Performance of the Concert Spiritual*, she cautions singers that "concert spirituals are not opportunities to show personal abandon without characterization and deference to style; neither are they modern gospel songs or German Lieder."[3] Originally, these songs were created by enslaved people and passed down through oral transmission primarily for survival and communication. They combined a spiritual connection to their African ancestors while creating new faith traditions in America to cope with their inhumane treatment, keeping hope alive for deliverance from the brutality of enslavement. Grappling with this history is a difficult but vital part of learning spiritual arrangements.

What we sing today with highly organized and systematic notation for concert performance is quite different from how these spirituals were used during slavery, when they served as functional music in everyday activities for survival and upliftment. That being said, in introducing this repertoire to a broader audience, the intentionality of the performance practice must always be front and center. Singers must be steeped in the historical context and musical genre to deliver a meaningful, respectful performance, especially when crossing the color barrier. In the preface to *The Books of the American Negro Spirituals*, James Weldon Johnson wrote:

> I think White singers, concert singers, can sing spirituals—if they feel them. But to feel them, it is necessary to know the truth about their origin and history, to get in touch with the association of ideas that surround them, and to realize something of what they meant in the experiences of the people who created them. In a word, the capacity to feel these songs while singing them is more important than any amount of mere artistic technique. Singers who take the spirituals as mere "art" songs and singers who make them an exhibition of what is merely amusing or exotic are doomed to failure, as far as true interpretation is concerned.[4]

As we enter the Black space with cultural humility, context, and respect, we must understand the intentionality of the music and those cultural bearers who brought these spirituals into existence, thereby continuing the tradition of the communicative power of African American spirituals to move hearts and express the Divine within humanity.

Black Theology

Even though the concert spirituals today do not sound like the folk spirituals sung during enslavement, the legacy of the folk tradition honors the ancestors who brought this music to America. Black theology is an essential lens for understanding the purpose of singing these religious folk melodies since they were not originally intended as concert pieces. In connecting spirituality in Black culture and critical race theory to the performance of concert spirituals, theologian James Cone (1970) provided a context for racial and cultural understanding within Christianity. Cone stated, "The black religious experience is something more than a black patina on a white happening. It is a unique response to a historical occurrence which can never be replicated for any people in America."[5] He commented further:

> It is not that Black Theology denies the importance of God's revelation in Christ, but Black people want to know what Christ means when they are confronted with the brutality of White racism . . . what does revelation mean

when one's being is engulfed in a system of White racism cloaking itself in pious moralities . . . what does God mean when a police officer whacks you over the head because you are Black?[6]

Black religious music, specifically plantation spirituals, "were depicted as unique in their emotive intensity. Abolitionists comprehended them as credible and honest testimonies, and they served as evidence to the newly admitted idea that slaves were possessors of spiritual depth, and authors and makers of meanings."[7] Biblical references in the spirituals stem from inspiring and influential s/heroes, such as Moses, Jesus, Elijah, Joshua, Samson, Noah, Daniel, and Mary, whose faith had been tested amid conflict. Enslaved communities echoed the words of "Elijah Rock" and "Joshua Fit de Battle O' Jericho" while they formed a blended (African and American) religious identity that fueled strength, courage, and justice in response to oppression, but also expressed a range of reactions from resistance to optimism through spirituals, such as "Cert'nly Lord (or Have You Got Good Religion?)" and "I Got A Robe."

Notes on Performance Practice

In the case of concert spirituals, historical context, personal intention, inspiration, and interpretative expression are the pillars of respectful performance practice. For them to have a significant impact, the performer must demonstrate proficiency in the source material as well as a contemporary understanding of performance practice in the twenty-first century. Composers H.T. Burleigh (1866–1949), Hall Johnson (1888–1970), and Roland Hayes (1887–1977) were practicing performers, either as singers or choral directors, in addition to being accomplished composers, and their experiences in both capacities are reflected in the performer-friendly nature of their compositions. At the same time, each heard spirituals sung by ex-slaves, creators of the original folk songs, and they brought the unfiltered purity of that exposure into the musical expression of their compositions.[8] The creation of the spiritual arrangements was not merely helpful but imperative, since they were bound by no rules before they were preserved in art song collections. Although the spirituals are classified under "religious songs," all are by no means religious in a narrow or particular sense, neither are they all songs of worship, even though they have a religious origin in usage. In the spirituals, the enslaved communities did express their religious hopes and fears, along with their faith and doubts. In each utterance of the spiritual, we hear the theological and ethical views of enslavement along with angst and warnings as well.

All singers, but especially those less familiar with these songs, must prepare for the performance of concert spirituals, bearing in mind that when we sing spiritual arrangements, there are distinctions between this genre and that of gospel as well as other types of African American music. Similarly, preparing to perform a concert spiritual includes independent research, study, and practice.[9] Here are a few items to consider when respectfully approaching the performance of concert spirituals:

1. Perform concert spirituals as written and avoid taking excessive liberties beyond what is in the score. Remember that concert spirituals are not the same as gospel music.
2. Pay close attention to the dialect if it is composed. Please do not change or overdo the pronunciation because both would destroy the composition's intent.
3. When using dialect, the singer(s) should remember to find the stresses and soften the final consonants "d" or "t." If you feel comfortable, performers may substitute Black vernacular (dialect) for common English words in an arrangement. For example, "the," "this," and "that" may become "de," "dis," and "dat" in dialect. "De" is usually pronounced "dee" before vowels and "duh" before consonants. The real purpose of the dialect is to honor the vernacular language, which produces a smoother transition between the words to avoid disruption of phrasing by excessive consonants. After you have worked on the nuances, tonal language (diction and/or dialect), and textual interpretation, you are ready to present these songs to the public.
4. Educate your audience (non–African American singers may need to explain or write program notes to discuss their preparation and affinity for spiritual arrangements).
5. And remember, sing these songs with your sensibility. Your voice and emotional connection to the music must shine through during the performance. Keep it sincere and honest!

In approaching the interpretation of concert spirituals, it is important to note that there are three distinct compositional categories of spirituals. The first category describes the slow, sustained spiritual with long, lyrical, and melodic phrases, such as "Deep River," "Give Me Jesus," and "Steal Away to Jesus." Some of these songs are categorized as "sorrow songs" due to their tonality and melancholic settings that use the pentatonic (five-tone) scale or minor mode, such as "Sometimes I Feel Like a Motherless Child," "City Called Heaven," and "Nobody Knows the Trouble I've Seen." These songs are incredibly moving ("soulful") and generally hypnotic because of the intense, sincere expression. They require singers to go beyond the music and reach deep within themselves to find the emotional and aesthetic capital necessary to sing "impressively well." As Burleigh once said, "Success in singing these folk songs primarily depends upon deep spiritual feeling. The voice is not nearly so important as the spirit; and then the rhythm, for the Negro's soul is linked with rhythm, and it is an essential characteristic of most all the folk songs."[10] Historically, some sorrow songs express a belief in the eventual deliverance from slavery, such as "Balm in Gilead" and "Over My Head." At the same time, some of these spirituals contained coded messages of escape routes to freedom, such as "Swing Low, Sweet Chariot," and "Wade in de Water."

The second category is up-tempo, shout-style spirituals, which contain highly rhythmic, syncopated notes with repeated melodic patterns and rousing choruses. Shout-style spirituals (sometimes termed "jubilees") contain short phrases with melodies full of syncopation and rhythmic vitality. This group of spirituals is generally popular for closing choral concerts and solo recitals and incorporating religious community gatherings. Some examples include "Ain-a Dat Good News," "Elijah Rock," Witness," "Ride On, King Jesus," and "Ev'ry Time I Feel the Spirit."

The last major category includes those arrangements of spirituals that use the "call and response" form. This type is shown in both slow and moderately fast tempos, with the leader (soloist) calling and the chorus responding. This song form is popular in many communities, including the African diaspora and beyond. Examples include "Go Down Moses," "Cert'nly Lord," and "I Got A Robe." Furthermore, some call and response spirituals also serve in subcategories such as traveling spirituals ("Swing Low, Sweet Chariot," "Ezekiel Saw de Wheel," and "I Want to Be Ready [to walk in Jerusalem just like John]").

Concert Spiritual Settings: Case Studies across Time and Styles

Even though various composers may arrange the melodic tune of any spiritual, these arrangements are given new musical treatment according to each composer's musical tastes and ideas of textual interpretation from indigenous source music. It is customary that the emergence of spiritual arrangements today in various styles honor the pioneering work of H.T. Burleigh, Nathaniel Dett, J. Rosamond Johnson, and Hall Johnson, among others, and continue the tradition. We will also honor the work of influential early composers as we explore two frequently performed traditional spirituals, "Ride On, King Jesus," and "Deep River," and compare two versions of each in order to appreciate the unique musical choices made by the composers.

Two Arrangements of "Ride On, King Jesus":
H.T. Burleigh and Hall Johnson

"Ride On, King Jesus" is a triumphant, life-affirming spiritual proclaiming that King Jesus (a supernatural emancipator of those oppressed) is indeed "King of Kings" and "Lord of Lords," and has the power to perform miracles or metaphysical acts, such as crossing the Jordan River, riding in the "middle of the air," and raising the dead. Even if you are not a believer, a singer must internalize all these things to interpret and become believable on stage and express the story clearly. The enslaved people often adopted biblical figures to help them, "not only as heroes but as ancestors to replace the African ancestors from whom they had been torn."[11]

Singer-composer Harry T. Burleigh (1866–1949) translated the unadorned folk spirituals from enslavement—which were not intended for performance, but rather communication, inspiration, emotional release, and survival—into art songs for the concert stage.[12] Even though people recognize Burleigh's major contribution to America's repository of concert spiritual arrangements for voice and piano, he was also well-known for his classical art songs. He is among the early American composers who wrote for singers, including legendary Black and White artists who promoted the Black spiritual genre (as opposed to White spirituals) during the early to mid-twentieth century, such as soprano Eileen Farrell (1920–2002), tenor John McCormack (1884–1945), tenor Roland Hayes (1887–1977), contralto Marian Anderson (1897–1993), bass-baritone Paul Robeson (1898–1976), baritone Todd Duncan (1903–1998), and many more. Burleigh published his dignified and majestic arrangement of "Ride On, King Jesus" in *The Spirituals of Harry T. Burleigh*, consisting of 203 pages for both high and low voices, a songbook that is a staple in many voice studios. He originally wrote "Ride On, King Jesus" as an SATB choral arrangement, but later created a setting for solo voice and piano in 1929.[13] Burleigh's setting of fifty-three measures of music is presented in a stately, march tempo from the maestoso beginning that sets up the main chorus or theme, "Ride On, King Jesus." Since Burleigh was a successful singer, his arrangements are extremely lyrical and accessible for beginners to professional singers, although some songs require advanced breath management and resonance balance. This particular arrangement demands a commanding presence, both vocally and physically on stage, in order to deliver the exhilarating message of the spiritual, especially with the declamatory approach on "Ride On, King Jesus."

The arrangement is in modified strophic form with a returning refrain ("Ride On, King Jesus"). The accompaniment is chordal (similar to hymn arrangements) and fully supports the lyrical melody, often doubling the voice part which uses the pentatonic (five-note) scale.[14] Burleigh uses some

Figure 6.1. Marian Anderson
Library of Congress, Van Vechten Collection, 1940 LCCN 2004662515 tif #49.

Figure 6.2. Harry T. Burleigh
Schomburg Center for Research in Black Culture, Jean Blackwell Hutson Research and Reference Division, The New York Public Library. "Harry T. Burleigh; Photo by Mishkin, New York." New York Public Library Digital Collections. Accessed January 15, 2023. https://digitalcollections.nypl.org/items/510d47dd-d7cb-a3d9-e040-e00a18064a99.

Black vernacular such as "ribber" for river, "almos'" for almost, "can-a" for can, and also engages a swinging syncopated rhythm at times, retaining the syncopated rhythms of the original spiritual.[15] Another interesting facet of Burleigh's setting is that there are two verses that use the "call and response" song form—a standard part of the African American tradition.[16] In the first verse, "King Jesus rides a milk-white horse," Burleigh uses sequencing with quarter and eighth note block chords in the accompaniment. In the second verse, we hear some lovely reharmonizing of the piano accompaniment in mm. 30–38 that provides a contrast to the straightforward and rhythmically moving choruses, delineating two distinct storytelling sections. The harmonic structure in this spiritual is less complex than in Burleigh's art songs and is entirely diatonic for the first half with a few hints of chromatic material in the second half of the song. The dynamics are mainly *mf* to begin the chorus and *p* on the verse "But now my race is almost done__no man can-a hinder me" before returning to the chorus ("Ride On, King Jesus").[17] There is a final allargando ("No man can-a hinder me") before a triumphant ending on the final words, "Ride! Ride! Ride!" Each one builds in intensity with dynamics from *f*, *ff*, to *sfz* until the last "Ride," held over two-tied whole notes to one-eighth note for a lasting dramatic effect, perhaps to convey eternity. This arrangement is published in both high and low keys.

Figure 6.3. Hall Johnson
Box 56, Harmon Foundation, Inc. Records, Manuscript Division, Library of Congress, Washington, DC.

Composer, conductor, and violinist Hall Johnson (1888–1949) was a trailblazer in both classical and non-classical vocal genres. His outstanding work on large-scale productions during the first part of the twentieth century included contributions to film that featured the Hall Johnson Choir, such as soundtracks for Frank Capra's *Lost Horizon*, Walt Disney's *Snow White and the Seven Dwarfs*, and Hal Roach's *Zenobia*. He also wrote and directed the music drama, *Run, Little Chillun*, which premiered on Broadway in 1933 and was the first Broadway show with an African American director and composer.[18] Additionally, he wrote art songs and spiritual arrangements for voice and piano. Hall Johnson's setting of "Ride On, King Jesus" is slightly different from Burleigh's but uses the same triumphant melodic material.

Dr. Eugene Thamon Simpson, executor for the Hall Johnson Estate and founding curator of the Hall Johnson Collection, wrote the book, *The Hall Johnson Spirituals: An Annotated Guide to Interpretation and Performance*. Since Dr. Simpson was a friend and protégé of the composer, it is an invaluable resource for any singer or pianist interested in programming and respectfully performing Hall Johnson's spirituals. "Ride On, King Jesus" is included in Simpson's book, and the author adds meticulous instructions by Hall Johnson on tempo, dynamic, formal structure, rhythm, diction, interpretation, and expression. For example, Johnson says the following:

> This song is a march, a triumphal march. Except for the *rallentando* followed by a long pause on the last page, the tempo must be mathematically strict throughout, with a steady rhythmic pulse. This effect can be achieved only by a particularly vigorous consonant on every beat, especially in the *pianissimo* passages. The second syllable of the word "Jesus" must be pronounced "zuss," (to rhyme with "fuss") even when it comes on a short note and especially when approaching the long pause. The dialect article "the" is always pronounced "dee" before vowels and "duh" before consonants. At the tempo marking "faster" (last 7 measures), count one to a measure and keep strict tempo to the end of the song, releasing the final "zuss" quite forcibly at the exact place indicated.[19]

The elements of rhythmic vitality and musical drive in Hall Johnson's arrangement of "Ride On, King Jesus" were inspired by Black idioms (jazz, blues, folk) as well as the Black vernacular, and his score is very meticulously marked. As noted, Johnson's attention to performance details is a key component for those interested in singing his arrangements, and the piano accompaniment requires a collaborative pianist with an excellent ear for sudden tempo and dynamic changes as well as navigating syncopated rhythms with varied articulations. The independence of the accompaniment and vocal parts creates an exciting and interactive ensemble experience since some thematic material appears both in the vocal and piano parts.[20] For example, there is a rap-like, conversational quality ("For he is King of Kings, Lord of Lords") embedded with a triumphant ending of four climactic "Ride On" responses. In interpreting the metaphysical elements of this spiritual, the performer must embrace representations of Jesus "riding a milk-white horse in the middle of the air" and "de ribber of Jerdin he did cross" (by foot, mind you), which depicts the appearance of Jesus as a towering supernatural figure. Johnson uses a wider vocal range and timbral palette than Burleigh does in his setting, with greater degrees of syncopation and motivic development, and he goes further in the piano accompaniment as well, with word painting of the "milk-white" horse in the bouncy accompaniment to that text. Johnson pulls out all the stops to bring the spiritual home with a big finish in tempo and dynamics on the repeated words "Ride on, ride on, ride on, Jesus." With increased dynamics on each repetition, from *forte* to *fortissimo*, there is a thrilling accelerando to the final long sustained note on the word "Jesus."

Comparative Texts between the Burleigh and Johnson Arrangements[21]

Burleigh

Chorus
Ride on King Jesus!
No man can-a hinder me.
Ride on, King Jesus, ride on!
No man can-a hinder me.

Verse 1
I was but young when I begun, No man can-a hinder me;
But now my race is almos' done, No man can-a hinder me.

Verse 2
King Jesus rides a milk-white horse, No man can-a hinder me;
De ribber of Jordan He did cross, No man can-a hinder me.

Johnson

Chorus
Ride on King Jesus!
No man can-a hinder me.
Ride on, King Jesus, ride on!
No man can-a hinder me.

Verse 1
King Jesus rides a milk-white horse, No man works like Him.

De ribber of Jerdin He did cross, No man works like Him.
For He is King of kings, Lord of Lords, Oh, Jesus Christ, de first an' las,' Oh!

Verse 2
King Jesus rides in de middle o' de air, Oh!
He calls de saints from everywhere, Ah!!

Chorus
Ride on King Jesus!
No man can-a hinder me.
Ride on, King Jesus, ride on!
No man can-a hinder me.
He is de King, He is de Lord, Ha!
Jesus Christ, de first an' las', No man works like Him!
Ride on, ride on, ride on, ride on, Jesus!

Two Arrangements of "Deep River": J. Rosamond Johnson and Moses Hogan

"Deep River" is an anonymous spiritual of African American origin that first appeared in *The Story of the Jubilee Singers: With Their Songs*, published by J.B.T. Marsh in 1876. This beloved, moving melody requires a sincere and emotionally invested singer who explores the text with interpretative skill in order to elucidate the transformative meaning. Eileen Guenther adds in her book, *In Their Own Words: Slave Life and the Power of Spirituals*, that "the symbolism of crossing 'over into campground' has more than one meaning—returning to Africa; escaping over the Ohio River, the Red River, any other river, really, or the Mason-Dixon Line; or going to heaven."[22] "Deep River" expresses hope and longing, using the river as a metaphor for passing over toward peace, and ultimately, freedom in the present as well as the afterlife. Through this song narrative, the melody and text resonate today for all those who seek refuge and hope.

Deep river,
My home is over Jordan.
Deep river, Lord.
I want to cross over into campground. Deep River,
My home is over Jordan.

Oh, don't you want to go,
To the Gospel feast;
That Promised Land,
Where all is peace?
Oh, deep river, Lord,
I want to cross over into campground.

94 ~ Chapter Six

Figure 6.4. James Weldon Johnson
Library of Congress, Van Vechten Collection, 1940 LCCN 2004662515 tif #49.

As we examine the arrangements of "Deep River," African American theologian and civil rights activist Howard Thurman (1899–1981) has provided an illuminating historical context to inspire singers, voice teachers, and collaborative pianists to create culturally relevant performances.

> ["Deep River"] is perhaps the most universal in insight and certainly the most intellectual of all the spirituals. In a bold stroke, it thinks of life in terms of a river. Of course, it must be added that to these early singers—slaves as they were—practically the river may have been for many the last and most formidable barrier to freedom. To slip over the river from one of the border states would mean a chance for freedom in the North—or, to cross the river into Canada would mean freedom in a new country, a foreign land. But let us reflect on a deeper meaning here. To think of life as being like a river is a full and creative analogy.[23]

J. Rosamond Johnson: "Deep River" (1925)[24]

Born in Jacksonville, Florida, J. (John) Rosamond Johnson (1873–1954) was most noted as the composer of the hymn "Lift Every Voice and Sing" with his older brother James Weldon Johnson, a gifted American poet,

Figure 6.5.   J. Rosamond Johnson
Box 56, Harmon Foundation, Inc. Records, Manuscript Division, Library of Congress, Washington, DC.

author, and civil rights activist. That composition, with its powerful text and rousing music, was dubbed the Black National Anthem and adopted as the official song of the National Association for the Advancement of Colored People in 1919. In addition, J. Rosamond Johnson, who attended the New England Conservatory before his desire for more musical training took him to London, was a multifaceted artist whose career included show business and performance tours on the vaudeville circuit. He and his brother also started a theatrical company with the noted African American actor, director, and composer Bob Cole (1868–1911). The following quote from James Weldon Johnson in the preface of their first book of spirituals is enlightening in terms of what they valued in their spiritual arrangements:

> In the arrangements, Mr. Rosamond Johnson and Mr. (Lawrence) Brown have been true not only to the best traditions of the melodies but also to form. No changes have been made in the form of songs. The only development has been in harmonizations, and these harmonizations have been kept true in character. . . . They have not been cut up or "opera-ated" upon. The arrangers have endeavored above all else to retain their primitive "swing." This collection is offered with the hope that it will further endear these songs to those who love spirituals, and will awaken an interest in many others.[25]

J. Rosamond Johnson adapted "Deep River" from the original version of the Fisk Jubilee Singers and was influenced by that choral tradition. His forty-six-measure setting in E-major is included in *The Books of American Negro Spirituals* (two volumes in one) by James Weldon Johnson and J. Rosamond Johnson. The emergence of broken chords in the piano introduction suggests the water movement in the river before the voice enters on "Deep river." In contrast to most settings of "Deep River," in which the song begins at a soft dynamic level, Johnson indicates a *mf* dynamic in the beginning for the piano and voice parts ("Deep river, my home is over Jordan") and then moves to *mp* on "Deep river, Lord, I want to cross over into campground." Singers who perform this setting are encouraged to find a variety of interpretive ways (such as toggling dynamics between *ppp* and *mf*) to bring this incredible melody, full of metaphysical reference, to life. African American Vernacular English is scarcely used here, only deliberately on the word, "chillun." On the last "Lord, I want to cross over into campground," the voice slowly and gradually dies away.

J. Rosamond Johnson's arrangement

Deep river, my home is over Jordan,
Deep river, Lord, I want to cross over into campground.
Lord, I want to cross over into campground, Lord,

I want to cross over into campground, __
I want to cross over into campground.
Oh, chillun,
Oh, don't you want to go, __ to that gospel feast,
That promised land, that land, where all is peace?
Walk into heaven, and take my seat, and cast my crown at Jesus feet Lord,
I want to cross over into campground, Lord,
I want to cross over into campground, __
I want to cross over into campground.
Deep river, my home is over Jordan,
Deep river Lord, I want to cross over into campground.
Lord, I want to cross over into campground,
Lord, I want to cross over into campground,
Lord, I want to cross over into campground, Lord!

Moses Hogan: "Deep River" (2000)[26]

With over seventy published works, the internationally renowned African American pianist, conductor, composer, and arranger Moses Hogan (1957–2003) was best known for his concert as well as choral spiritual settings. Moses Hogan directed the Moses Hogan Singers and toured extensively in the United States and abroad. His arrangements are widely known and popular for high school, college, church, community, and professional choirs worldwide.

The text for the traditional spiritual, "Deep River," is based on Joshua 3 from the Bible. Moses Hogan's forty-four-measure setting is in the *Deep*

Figure 6.6. Moses Hogan
https://www.singers.com/choral/director/Moses-Hogan/.

River Collection: Ten Spirituals arranged for solo voice and piano. In an understandable contrast to J. Rosamond Johnson's "Deep River," Hogan's setting employs a contemporary harmonic palette, drawing from jazz and gospel styles, and including seventh chords and suspensions. It begins with a whole note pedal tone (Eb2 in the high key and C2 in the low) before it unfolds harmonically with influences from Black vernacular music traditions. In another nod to those vernacular traditions, Hogan uses the device of humming at the end of the first chorus and on the song's last note after the phrase, "I want to cross over into campground," evoking a very personal experience on the part of the singer. This version begins *mp* on the first utterance of "Deep river, my home is over Jordan," then moves to *mf* before increasing to *f* ("Oh, don't you want to go, to that gospel feast"). Hogan's arrangement continues to intensify with broader phrasing until the highest note of the piece is sounded on "that promised land" before settling down to *mp* to *p* at the conclusion, "where all is peace," and "Deep river, Lord, I want to cross over into campground."

Hogan's arrangement

Deep river, my home is over Jordan.
Deep River, Lord, I want to cross over into campground.
Hm._____
Deep river, my home is over Jordan.
Deep River, Lord, I want to cross over into campground.
Oh, don't you want to go,___ to that gospel feast,
That promised land where all is peace.
Deep river, Lord, I want to cross over into campground. Hm.

Creators from the African diaspora combined music idioms they encountered in the United States with African traditions, producing a blended culture and resulting in a rich body of song, deeply rooted in historical context and tradition. In an effort to maintain and honor its relevance, African American composers later "elevated" the spiritual through classical settings for the concert hall, but in the next section, we will explore how that relevance extends even more strongly to non-classical genres of American vocal music.

Spirituals as a Path to Non-Classical Genres in the Voice Studio

Vocal training in the academy is rapidly evolving and expanding in the twenty-first century. Because of demand, many voice departments in universities and colleges are rushing to expand their offerings to include musical theatre and popular music programs or add minor concentrations. While classical voice teachers are sometimes reluctant to confront these curricular changes, we could use this moment of cultural disruption as a unique opportunity to tailor our teaching and connect to a more diverse group of students using spiritual settings as a bridge to non-classical genres. Conversely, voice teachers in musical theatre or contemporary commercial music can become more conscious of the role spirituals have played as the bedrock of American popular songwriting, explicitly naming African American contributions to all the genres and repertoire used to train their students.

The seminal relationship between spirituals and American song has long been recognized by Black and White writers, historians, and pedagogues. In 1932, W.E.B. Du Bois wrote that

> the slaves originated this curious and beautiful volume of song that has come down through centuries as a never-to-be-forgotten contribution to the world's music. From it has developed the "gospel" hymns of the Whites, the syncopated rhythm and jazz of the world of art and a wealth of material for great composers like Henry Franklin Belknap Gilbert (1868-1928) and Antonin Dvořák (1841-1904).[27]

In 2016, this connection was explicitly acknowledged by the National Association of Teachers of Singing, the largest professional association of teachers of singing in the world, through its addition of a Hall Johnson Spirituals prize to its annual district and regional voice competitions in order "to encourage excellence and authenticity in the performances of America's most significant indigenous contribution to music, The Spiritual—the progenitor of Ragtime, Jazz, Gospel, Swing, Rock and Roll, Blues, Soul Music, and Hip Hop."[28] American popular song has arguably had a much greater global impact and reach than American classical composers' contributions to concert repertoire, which begs the question, why do we insist that only a particular song repertoire is beneficial for effectively teaching voice? What can we learn from other musical styles that inform our pedagogies while meeting students from diverse musical backgrounds? Suppose we encounter a student with a significant jazz or gospel background. How would we engage that particular student? What conversation would allow for teaching singing by function related to the non-classical repertoire? Voice students can learn from singing across styles in ways that provide a more inclusive learning environment, and voice teachers should be supported and encouraged to embrace their musical tastes through a non-classical Black music lens to begin balancing the canon.

Musical Theatre Meets Black Popular Song Genres

As we discussed in chapter 1, the globally popular and influential American art form of musical theatre arose from the American stage traditions of Blackface minstrelsy and vaudeville. Show tunes and popular song shared the same space in the first half of the twentieth century, as did the racial stereotyping and segregation that was enforced in the entertainment industry. Thus the contributions of Black songwriters to staged works in the commercial realm were strictly constrained to perpetuating those stereotypes, and when we look for foundational Black contributions to the genre, what we find is an output driven by economic and social constraints—"Realdramatik," if you will—to which some of the titles of the earliest works of Black musical theatre attest, such as Bob Cole's *A Trip to Coontown* (1898) and Eubie Blake and Noble Sissle's *Shuffle Along* (1921). And because of the realities of American racial segregation, what developed over the decades was an art form based on White (also predominantly male) composers writing for White audiences. However, the civil rights era made a creative shift in the direction of American musical theatre possible, and in the late 1960s and 1970s there were a variety of shows that drew on Black genres in popular music as well as Black themes, paving the way for the overriding creative trends we see in contemporary works for musical theatre. While this shift has revitalized the art form in many ways, it has also highlighted the need for a different approach to training the twenty-first-century musical theatre singer.

Musical theatre voice teachers face a host of challenges in the academy of today. First, many of us have been trained with the estimable skill set of the nineteenth-century opera singer, but we are required to meet the needs of preparing our students to succeed in the musical theatre world of the twenty-first century, in which contemporary works are based much more on popular music styles than the operetta-like singing of Golden Age repertoire. That being said, from the point of view of vocal training, good singing across popular song styles (from blues to gospel to jazz to soul and R&B to rock and pop) is defined by the same set of technical criteria that provides the foundation for classical singing: the singer needs to develop breath support for a stable and healthy vocal production; consistent, aesthetically pleasing, and stylistically appropriate tone quality; accurate intonation; dynamic control across the entire vocal range; intelligible diction; a technical foundation that enables legato phrasing and florid display; and the imaginative freedom to craft a dramatic characterization that drives an emotionally compelling performance. One only needs to listen to singers such as Ella Fitzgerald, Sammy Davis, Jr., Whitney Houston, and Audra McDonald (among so many others) to understand that true artistry cannot be defined solely through a classical lens. The challenge is to provide models of good singing across styles and to understand and respect the vocalism and musicianship required to become that kind of artist.

There are other challenges as well. As we seek to diversify the canon of musical theatre repertoire for our students, the task is not as simple as just performing theater music written by Black songwriters. In contrast to the problem presented by diversifying the canon of classic song, where the first barrier is *finding* the repertoire, with musical theatre we are faced with the fact that, although the songs are easily accessible, the songs themselves (as in the earlier examples) perpetuate racial stereotypes that are offensive. Additionally, the process of choosing roles for students to study and perform is fraught with special considerations that are constrained by historical performance practice, directorial casting choices, and audience expectations. However, by utilizing the ample resource of Black popular song to train our students, we can break through the barrier of musical theatre's racist roots and achieve the pedagogical outcome of positively representing an array of Black creative voices in our studio teaching. And because the practice of "covering" a song is widespread and familiar, we can make repertoire choices for our students that are unencumbered by casting conventions, providing students of all ethnic backgrounds with the vocal foundation to become successful contemporary musical theatre singers.

Case Studies in Popular Song: Learning Contemporary Musical Theatre Vocalism, Style, and Musicianship from the Greats of Jazz, R&B, Soul, and Gospel

Popular song defines our shared cultural space, as any trip to the grocery store will tell you if you're listening to the music over the loudspeakers while you shop. Even though many of us earn a living in the academy, which historically has not given much thought or credence to popular music, we all have imbibed through it the myriad contributions of African American creators and performers. Many of these performers turned to popular music genres because their classical aspirations were thwarted by racism; the great jazz singer and pianist Nina Simone (1933–2003), for example, aspired to a career as a concert pianist but was denied admission to the classical piano performance program at the Curtis Institute. As a result, she plowed her astounding musicianship into a career as a jazz pianist and singer that began in the 1950s in jazz clubs in New York City, and she went on to become a hugely influential recording artist and outspoken creative voice for civil rights. Other luminaries of popular song began their performing careers as children with little to no formal training, such as Stevie Wonder (a child prodigy), Aretha Franklin (singing gospel in her father's church), and Ella Fitzgerald, who first performed at the Apollo Theater when she was seventeen. In the following section, we will focus on these three legendary recording artists of the past century and consider how their artistry can guide the growing number of musical theatre students in voice studios across the country.

Jazz is a product of Black creativity and musical skill that is unparalleled in its influence on American popular song, not to mention Western art music of the twentieth century. One could create an entire course on the music of Duke Ellington and the artistry of Ella Fitzgerald, but we have chosen to focus on one iconic Duke Ellington song that was a standard in Ella Fitzgerald's repertoire: "It don't mean a thing (if it ain't got that swing)." The up-tempo tune has a rhythmic drive and energy that Fitzgerald epitomizes in her vocal rendition.[29] One important aspect of good rhythm is precision, and Fitzgerald is always in sync with the band in terms of tempo and drive—this is not a case of the band "following" the singer. In terms of her rhythmic as well as pitch precision, the skills necessary to execute an up-tempo song in jazz equate themselves to the requirements of singing the energetic and pointillistic songs of Stephen Sondheim, especially something like "On the steps of the palace" sung by Cinderella in *Into the Woods* or Mrs. Lovett's opening number in *Sweeney Todd*, "The Worst Pies in London." While scatting and improvisation are not typically called for in musical theatre, one can only stand back and admire Fitzgerald's grasp of harmony and playful melodic gesture while she lets the percussive syllables flow. But another aspect of her singing that maps very well onto musical theatre in general and Sondheim in particular is her fluid navigation of registration, with perfect evenness of tone from her chesty mix to her head voice, a skill that any singer would find indispensable when playing Dot in *Sunday in the Park with George*.

Stevie Wonder's sweet, high voice and expressive phrasing have been a part of America's soundtrack since the early 1960s when he first signed a contract with Motown records at the age of eleven. He is one of the best-selling recording artists of all time and has received twenty-five Grammy awards, among other accolades. His songwriting is creative and prolific, and he has been a leading influence in all styles of Black popular song, from R&B to funk and from gospel to soul. Using the song "Overjoyed" (which was released in 1985 on his album entitled *In Square Circle*) as an example, we observe that the tessitura is quite high, sung in what is referred to by contemporary musical theatre tenors as a "mix" tone of voice, and happens to epitomize the most sought-after voice type of male singing in contemporary musical theatre repertoire. His style of singing ranges from soft and sensitive to brilliant and bright, often managing a lot of text in a given phrase, which maps perfectly onto such contemporary leading man tenor roles as Pippin (*Pippin*) and Fiyero (*Wicked*) in musicals by Stephen Schwartz, and is also an excellent training ground for all the male roles in *Dear Evan Hansen* or *Dogfight* by Benj Pasek and Justin Paul.

Last but not least, we look to the Queen of Soul, Aretha Franklin, as a role model for contemporary female musical theatre singers. Franklin's vocal and expressive skills were honed singing gospel music in her father's church, and that style remained central to her vocalism in her pop and soul recordings.

One of the challenges of being a woman in the current musical theatre world is that you need to be able to sing in all styles, from Golden Age repertoire that for leading ladies is head register dominant and for the comic roles more chest register dominant, but also manage the vocal demands of mix and belt in the contemporary dramatic roles from such recent Broadway hits as *Dreamgirls*, *The Color Purple*, and *Six*. Franklin's gospel singing offers a model for the vocalism of these challenging roles with its range of expressive and sincere vocalism from soft to loud, and low to high, the upward extension of an emotionally powerful belt, and the flexibility to "riff" improvisationally while maintaining pinpoint intonation and rhythmic precision soloistically as well as in moments of ensemble singing. In a track from her gospel album *Amazing Grace*, Franklin performs a song that combines two beloved tunes, one gospel and one pop—"Precious Lord, Take My Hand/You've Got a Friend"—with mesmerizing dramatic flair in an arrangement that is echoed at various moments by the music of the Schuyler sisters in Lin-Manuel Miranda's groundbreaking musical *Hamilton*.

We encourage all voice teachers and their musical theatre students to spend some time doing YouTube deep dives on these three singers and many more, in an effort to acknowledge and appreciate the monumental Black artists of American popular song. The internet makes this kind of exercise so very easy and accessible, and students can hone their critical thinking skills by quantifying the technical prowess demonstrated by these legendary artists. Using African American popular song performers and creators as a guide, voice students can connect with and celebrate African American contributions to American song while developing their own artistry for their futures on the musical theatre stage.

Notes

1. Zora Neale Hurston, "Spirituals and Neo-Spirituals (1934)," in *The New Negro: Readings on Race, Representation, and African American Culture, 1892-1938*, edited by Henry Louis Gates and Gene Andrew Jarrett (Princeton: Princeton University Press, 2008), 473–74.

2. Please see "Selected Bibliography and Resources."

3. Cheryl Susheel Bibbs, *The Art of the Spiritual: Enhancing Performance of the Concert Spiritual* (Sacramento, CA: Daya Kay Communications, Inc., 2016), 35.

4. James Weldon Johnson and J. Rosamond Johnson, *The Books of American Negro Spirituals* (New York: Da Capo Press, 1973), 28–29.

5. J.H. Cone, *A Black Theology of Liberation* (New York: Lippincott, 1970), 8.

6. Cone, *A Black Theology of Liberation*, 54.

7. Jon Cruz, *Culture on the Margins: The Black Spiritual and the Rise of American Cultural Interpretation* (Princeton: Princeton University Press, 1999), 68.

8. Jones, *So You Want to Sing Spirituals*, 39–40.

9. Rosephanye Dunn-Powell, "The African-American Spiritual: Preparation and Performance Considerations," NATS *Journal of Singing* 61, no. 5 (May/June 2005): 469.

10. H.T. Burleigh, *The Spirituals of Harry T. Burleigh* (Rockville Centre, NY: Belwin Mills, 2001), 4.

11. M. Roger Holland, II, "Spirituals Radio Project: How a Grand Vision of Jesus on a White Horse Signaled Triumph over Slavery," April 19, 2021, https://www.cpr.org/2021/04/19/spirituals-radio-project-how-a-grand-vision-of-jesus-on-a-white-horse-signaled-triumph-over-slavery/.

12. Horowitz, *Dvořák's Prophecy*, 102.

13. Patricia Saunders Nixon, "Harry T. Burleigh's Art Songs: A Forgotten Repertory" (DMA dissertation, Shenandoah University, 2011), 80.

14. Nixon, "Harry T. Burleigh's Art Songs," 80–81.

15. Nixon, "Harry T. Burleigh's Art Songs," 80–81.

16. Nixon, "Harry T. Burleigh's Art Songs," 80–81.

17. Nixon, "Harry T. Burleigh's Art Songs," 80–81.

18. Southern, *The Music of Black Americans*, 421.

19. Eugene T. Simpson, *The Hall Johnson Concert Spirituals* (West Conshohocken, PA: Infinity Publishing, 2015), 102.

20. Simpson, *The Hall Johnson Concert Spirituals*, 106.

21. In each arrangement, the verses vary by each composer because verses were often passed down through oral transmission.

22. Eileen Morris Guenther, *In Their Own Words: Slave Life and the Power of Spirituals* (Saint Louis, MO: MorningStar Music Publishers, 2016), 87.

23. Howard Thurman, *Deep River and the Negro Spirituals Speak of Life and Death* (Richmond, IN: United Friends Press, 1975), 70.

24. Significance or Dedication: This spiritual arrangement is found in an edited two-volume *Book of American Negro Spirituals*, dedicated to American author, nineteenth-century intellectual, and educator Booker T. Washington. Washington was also the founder of the Tuskegee Normal and Industrial Institute (known as Tuskegee University) and the National Negro Business League.

25. Johnson, James Weldon, J. Rosamond Johnson, Lawrence Brown, and J. Rosamond (John Rosamond) Johnson. "The Book of American Negro Spirituals / Edited with an Introduction by James Weldon Johnson ; Musical Arrangements by J. Rosamond Johnson, Additional Numbers by Lawrence Brown." (New York: Viking Press, 1925.), 50.

26. Significance or Dedication: In honor of Edna Sampsong Hargett, commissioned by The Negro Spiritual Scholarship Foundation for the 1999 Grady-Rayam Prize in Sacred Music, Orlando, Florida.

27. Quoted in John Lovell, *Black Song: The Forge and the Flame; the Story of How the Afro-American Spiritual Was Hammered Out* (New York: Macmillan, 1972), 87.

28. Simpson, *The Hall Johnson Concert Spirituals*, 5.

29. See any of the clips turned up by a search on YouTube.

SECTION III

STRATEGIES FOR CREATING COMMUNITY AND BUILDING MUSIC ECOSYSTEMS

CHAPTER SEVEN

Allyship, Permission, and Informed Performance Practice

By engaging in the respectful study, performance, and advocacy of music by Black composers, we are responding within the United States and globally to the present moment. There is no one-size-fits-all model for building allyships, seeking permission from cultural bearers, and introducing pathways to informed performance practice. Whereas this book has emerged from our experiences, interactions with students, and our diverse circle of colleagues, we see our job as still evolving in the current socio-political climate. Therefore, we seek to invite all collaborative allies to the table who acknowledge the historical deficit of Black voices in classical music. Emery recently recalled a conversation with a high school classmate who wanted to know why he was interested in classical music. Emery's classmate thought classical music was a White genre since he was not aware of many Black classical musicians. Through a Black lens, anyone unfamiliar with the canon might assume and not necessarily identify classical music as a viable choice for a Black musician due to the lack of African American representation. But by educating audiences and non-musicians about the tremendous contributions of Black composers, we can now invite a more robust community of musicians to the classical concert stage and celebrate America's diverse musical soundscape. The following quote supports this precise idea in the book chapter "Industrializing African American Popular Music" by Reebee Garofalo:

> It is, by now, common knowledge that African Americans have provided the most significant cultural inputs in the development of American music. African Americans have created, innovated, performed, and otherwise

participated in the process of music-making since the United States was a colony. Their cultural contributions have been historically undervalued and/or assigned to others less deserving, and they have had to overcome systemic discrimination within the music industry itself. Still, the music remains as vital and pathbreaking as ever.[1]

This chapter discusses the unique contributions that people from varying ethnic backgrounds can make to reposition all the American voices within the song canon. Our research, teaching, and performance have identified multiple and complex barriers to diversifying the canon. However, issues of representation and race are so complicated in the United States that once any singer chooses to perform a song by a Black composer, they must often navigate uniquely American sociological truths, regardless of race. We can face these barriers by entering brave spaces with practical solutions in our institutions and private studios, providing an experience of communal permission to study and perform the repertoire of composers of African descent, which benefits us as artists through experiencing empathy for the people we're portraying and gaining a nuanced understanding of their lived experiences.

Allyship

Effective allyship is based on active listening skills and invites individuals to support other identities through opportunities that result from their power, positionality, or privilege. In the twenty-first century, conversations on race, influence, and representation occupy performance and classroom spaces among groups of people, requiring courage to lean into discomfort from the past. We must acknowledge that even a tiny action of allyship can help establish support. The *Cambridge Dictionary* defines "allyship" as "the quality or practice of helping or supporting other people who are part of a group that is treated badly or unfairly, although you are not a member of this group."[2]

Author Amélie Lamont shares in her guide on allyship that

> being an ally is hard work, and many would-be allies fear making mistakes that could have them labeled as "-ist" or "-ic" (racist, sexist, transphobic, homophobic, etc.). But as an ally, you're also affected by a system of oppression. This means that as an ally, there is much to unlearn and learn—mistakes are expected. You need to own this as fact and should be willing to embrace the daily work of doing better. As an ally, you need to own your mistakes and be proactive in your education every day. If you refuse to acknowledge that your words and actions are inherently shaped and influenced by systemic oppression, you're setting up yourself to fail.[3]

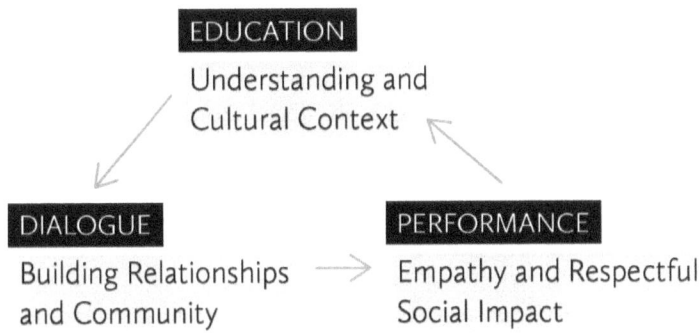

Figure 7.1. Education, Dialogue, and Performance
Stephens and Clark, 2023.

Allyship requires that all hands be on deck with eyes and ears wide open. This process-oriented relationship is often a lifelong pursuit that acknowledges that we are stronger together and learn from one another. Our cultural differences are celebrated and recognized among each group. However, the actual work must be proactive and involves patience, resilience, and willingness to listen and respond appropriately to differing views while speaking truth to power and changing the trajectory of events that have led to systemic exclusion. Allies need not worry about knowing all the answers, but they must enter the Black space with cultural humility, empathy, and respect. So what does allyship look like? It is a proactive commitment based on actions rather than a passive response to a given issue affecting an individual or community. In a *Forbes Magazine* article, "Allyship—The Key to Unlocking the Power of Diversity," Sheree Atcheson (Diversity, Equity, & Inclusion contributor) writes, "an ally is any person that actively promotes and aspires to advance the culture of inclusion through intentional, positive, and conscious efforts that benefit people as a whole. Everyone can be an ally, as privilege is intersectional. For example, White people can be actionable allies to people of color, and men can be allies to women."[4] The article further defines allyship as "1) a lifelong process of building relationships based on trust, consistency, and accountability with marginalized individuals and/or groups of people; 2) not self-defined—work and efforts must be recognized by those you are seeking to ally with, and 3) an opportunity to grow and learn about ourselves while building confidence in others."[5]

The term "allyship" has roots in the 1840s; however, the term has expanded to support racial justice and social barriers affecting marginalized or underrepresented groups. However, academic author Emma Dabri said that "Allyship offers charity whereas coalition is more about solidarity" and that allyship's emphasis on the efforts of a privileged group to help disadvantaged groups reflects a "paternalistic attitude." Even though we can read various interpretations of allyship, we are confident that allyship is making a difference and can provide substantive support for marginalized groups or individuals rather than a self-serving gesture.[6]

> Allyship is the lifelong process in which people with privilege and power work to develop empathy towards another marginalized group's challenges or issues. The goal of allyship is to create a culture in which the marginalized group feels valued, supported, and heard. Being an ally is not a label—it is a verb.[7]

> A true ally must regularly listen to those around them, adapt their thinking, rework what they believe to be correct & become comfortable being uncomfortable. It can be a unique and challenging journey becoming and remaining an ally, but certainly, one worth taking.[8]

As any action plan requires intentional discussion and reflection, please consider implementing the following suggestions:

1. Advocate for and support (time, influence, and financial resources) other groups and identities.
2. Give credit first to identities and causes you support.
3. Do not take criticism personally; lean into discomfort and do not respond abruptly—count to three slowly, and just wait and think about the best way and time to respond. Remember the LRR (Listen-Reflect-Respond) technique.
4. Tune into lived experiences of underrepresented people and self-reflect on how these stories impact work on diversity, equity, inclusion, and anti-racism.
5. Acknowledge power structures and systems beyond your control and follow up with constructive action steps.

Allyship can exist between individuals as well as institutions since communities can emerge through listening, support, self-reflection, and fostering systemic change. Agents of allyship are crucial, for example, to support emerging Black artists, performance projects, new compositions that tell culturally relevant stories, and interdisciplinary projects and partnerships. Music promoters; artist managers; recording studios; entrepreneurs; foundations funded by local, state, and federal grants; and private grantors are actively working to bring more diverse performances to venues and schools, but further work must be undertaken to define and establish best practices to foster allyship on an individual or institutional level.

Case Studies: Engaging Experts in the Field

One suggestion for successful allyship involves consultation with cultural bearers and music experts to learn about context, cultural awareness, and performance history and practice. It is a given that no one needs to enter this work alone when professional individuals and music organizations are willing to assist with your professional goals. During a summer research mentoring program, Emery had the pleasure to mentor two undergraduate researchers[9] who interviewed three experts and practitioners: Randye Jones, a vocal performer and music librarian; Reinaldo Moya, a composer; and music publisher Glendower Jones. These interviews were informative and provided an opportunity to learn the professional trajectories of music experts using the following questions to guide the conversations:

1. Describe your musical experiences thus far.
2. What are some of the barriers you encountered in your journey? How did you overcome them?
3. In the context of your work, what is being done to highlight historically marginalized voices? What more needs to be done?
4. You have significant experience as a guest speaker, panelist, and lecturer. As an educator, what question are you asked the most on that circuit?
5. Was there any specific point in your life that inspired you to start advocating for the voices of composers of color?

Randye Jones

Randye Jones is a performer, scholar, and educator currently serving as a media coordinator at Grinnell College in Iowa. She specializes in the research and performance of concert spirituals composed for solo vocalists. She has lectured and performed in venues throughout the country and recently published the book, *So You Want to Sing Spirituals*, in collaboration with the National Association of Teachers of Singing and Rowman &

Littlefield Publishers. Jones' next project is the discography *Recorded Solo Concert Spirituals, 1916-2022*, scheduled for publication in 2023. Her other work includes *The Spirituals Database*, a searchable database of spirituals with over 6200 entries, and *Afrocentric Voices in Classical Music*, a website with comprehensive profiles of several African American performers and composers and suggestions and resources for continuing education.

In her interview, Jones provided the following opinions and observations, describing the study and performance of spirituals as the duty of every American singer:

- Do not seek permission to sing spirituals. Feel the obligation to do so.
- Mastering the art of singing concert spirituals is as important for a performer's development as the study of any other style of singing. Students studying for a vocal performance or similar music degree must learn, program, and perform this music, regardless of their background.
- Performers must include a diverse body of works and styles within their repertoire to project the assertion that they are experienced, knowledgeable interpreters of art songs.
- To that end, the spiritual has influenced American music so heavily that it is nearly impossible to find an area that has not been at least indirectly affected. As an American musician, you need to connect with spirituals to build a deeper understanding of how other kinds of music have developed.
- Spirituals should be used to teach. Technical, artistic, and cultural skills are as necessary and teachable therein as they are in any other art song genre. Program pieces for their educational value, not simply because they check a box for inclusion or diversity.

> "My goal is to create easily accessible resources from the materials that have taken me decades to gather myself. I don't care whether you're Black or White. . . . I want you to have a thorough understanding of vocal music. The fact that you are not African American does not excuse you from having that contact."

—Randye Jones

Reinaldo Moya

Reinaldo Moya is a composer from Caracas, Venezuela, and as a child, he took part in El Sistema, a music education program that offers a musical experience to people of all ages and socioeconomic statuses in Venezuela. Being part of this program allowed him to play with Venezuela's Children's

Orchestra and tour with the Simon Bolivar Orchestra. In 1999, he emigrated to Maryland with his family, where he finished his high school education. He then received his bachelor's degree in music from West Virginia University and completed his master's and doctoral degrees at The Juilliard School. He has received several fellowships, including the Charles Ives Fellowship from the American Academy of Arts and Letters, the 2015 McKnight Composers Fellowship, the Van Lier Fellowship from *Meet the Composer*, and the Aaron Copland Award from the Copland House. The *Star Tribune* applauded his chamber opera *Tienda* for its "proud individuality . . . [and] textures of pulsing vibrancy, subtly shading harmonies to trace the fragile emotional arc of his central characters." He has taught at St. Olaf College and Interlochen Arts Camp and is currently an associate professor of composition at Augsburg University in Minneapolis.

The interview with Dr. Moya included the following insights:

> Music can be a big help when experiencing a change in our lives. When Reinaldo immigrated to the US, music helped him with that transition because even though everything in his life was different, "orchestra was the same." He continued, saying, "it didn't matter if I didn't understand English at that point or if my English was not where I needed it to be, I could just pick up my violin and play alongside everybody else, and that made me feel a sense of belonging." One of the main barriers composers of color experience is knowing if their music is programmed because it is valuable work or just to fulfill the diversity requirement. No matter how you culturally identify yourself, music is for everyone! However, it is essential to research before playing a piece by a composer of color.
>
> > "We make art because we want to communicate . . . if the only people who are allowed to sing my music are other Latinos, we're missing out on the most powerful thing performers can do . . . it's about being able to experience life through other people's experiences."
>
> —Reinaldo Moya

Glendower Jones

Glendower Jones is a musician, printer, and publisher based in Fayetteville, Arkansas. His music business, Classical Vocal Reprints (CVR), is responsible for producing, storing, and distributing thousands of scores yearly. He has consistently used his position to advocate for historically marginalized composers. As a young adult, he played the trombone, sang with the Saint Thomas Choir in New York, and worked at the Joseph Patelson Music House before starting CVR in 1987. As a music dealer, he orders from other publishers and resells music, but he also serves as a publisher who works with living composers. He prints anthologies, engravings, textbooks, octavos, and, by his assessment, just about anything else that comes across his desk. Glendower has routinely pushed for increased awareness of women composers and composers of color through publishing, programming, and study, and CVR's website offers evidence of his tireless work. His recent publication is *An Anthology of African and African Diaspora Songs*, edited by Louise Toppin and Scott Piper.

The interview with Glendower Jones yielded the following surprising information:

- For much of the twentieth century, no one would even consider publishing the music that CVR is now regularly distributing. A publisher might have been ready to finalize a deal, discovered that the composer was Black, and rescinded the offer. The publishing industry has intentionally and systematically excluded certain groups in favor of older white men. They have a great deal of power over deciding what music will comprise the canon, and often, there are only one or two individuals in charge of what is published and what is not.
- Several international publishing companies own the rights to large quantities of music by historically marginalized composers, but these companies won't take the time to publish the works. The result is that no one can have it because copies just don't exist, and if someone wanted to purchase the rights so that they could perform and reproduce it, the costs are prohibitive. When we talk about the lack of access to music by composers of color, this is often the root of the problem.
- Vocal, dedicated individuals must research, compile, publish, publicize, and purchase music, but anyone can take on those roles. You can take on those roles! Explore the CVR website and explore new publications—the information has never been so readily available as it is today.

Lifelong Education and the Role of Cultural Humility

"No culture over time has existed without a belief system to underpin and sustain it. No art can survive without an understanding of and dedication to the values and vision of its creators."[10]

—William C. Banfield, Professor Emeritus of Africana Studies and Music and Society, Berklee College of Music"

As we examine ways to decenter Western European repertoire and cultivate American music-making beyond classical, we have a tremendous opportunity to redesign and reimagine our music curricula and teaching philosophies to serve various traditions in American music. In 2016, the College Music Society published a report, "Transforming Music Study from its Foundations: A Manifesto for Progressive Change in the Undergraduate Preparation of Music Majors," which urges readers "to overcome the inertia of established programs and cultures dominated by interpretive performance and study of European classical music, a new integrated program—replete with creativity and diversity and still including the treasures of European heritage—will require not only curricular overhaul but new ways of thinking conversing, and forging strategic initiatives."[11] According to Ladson-Billings (1994), culturally responsive teaching is "a pedagogy that empowers students intellectually, socially, emotionally, and politically [because it uses] cultural referents to impart knowledge, skills, and attitudes."[12] Furthermore, engaging in student-centered pedagogy often invites the exploration of ethnic music traditions outside of Eurocentrism in higher education.

Cultural humility deals with preconceptions, assumptions, and biases through self-exploration and reflection. Although many prejudices and biases are formed early in a person's development, many schools have responded by implementing more intentional plans regarding diversity and equity through activities, guest speakers, curricula examination, focus groups, and hiring staff and administrators to lead the institutional efforts to address race, equity, anti-racism, and belonging. We must remember to reflect on our background and the background of others while teaching, learning, conducting research, performing, and leading culturally relevant performances. How do we view cultural humility in music diversity? What are the respective points of entry? No doubt about it—education matters deeply in this endeavor. In many cases of establishing effective allyship, people may need to realize their unique privilege or how to use their influence to help others respectfully. The most challenging part of group discussions involves listening to others who have experienced bias, systemic racism, exclusion, and microaggressions. But since the positionality of allies emerges from membership in a privileged group, starting from this point of awareness makes it possible to establish a space in which to build trust and identify shared goals.

Permission and Shared Responsibility

When does consent happen? Who permits us? Permission is usually given when the requestor builds trust with the cultural bearers, takes the time to learn and honor the performance practice, and gives proper credit to the inventors (i.e., communities or individuals who are allies and collaborators on specific artistic projects). Therefore, when preparing to perform work from a culture outside your own, cultural context and sensitivity play a significant role in establishing any performer's credibility and believability. Conversely, discussing your intentionality in performing work is crucial since we are responsible for telling someone else's story from another culture. And while the willingness to be a part of the solution is essential, allyship in a performance setting may only prove effective when approached with careful consideration and education. The non-Black performer may face criticism, which is difficult to experience, but true allies invite that criticism, explain their reasoning, engage with feedback, and reposition their efforts as needed to move forward.

In terms of shared responsibility, we should bear in mind that everyone ultimately benefits through allyship in reciprocal relationships, where the participants are connected through mutual respect and linked by a common cause or purpose. In establishing integrated communities to share the responsibility of advocating for restoring Black voices to the canon, we center the Black voice within American stories that have so often been told as if only "White" music had value. And when audiences get used to seeing diverse groups of performers honoring and giving life to songs by African American creators, centering Black song can become normalized among performers of all races.

Informed Performance Practice

When performing songs by Black composers in any genre, especially those that reference the experience of being African American, one needs to be very conscious of the usage of signifying musical or linguistic compositional elements. Composers rarely make choices that don't carry meaning, and performers must make an effort to understand the cultural references in all their complexity and depth. There are so many ways to convey meaning with a song, both consciously and unconsciously, because the combination of text and music gives both information and emotion, and even music alone provides a subtext that can point to very specific historical moments or deliver biting social commentary. The tools that an African American composer brings to the table range from the most obvious signifier of Blackness, that of language—specifically African American Vernacular English—to Black vernacular musical genres—such as spirituals, blues, jazz, or gospel—in rhythmic choices, harmonizations, or vocal stylization. All singers are trained to do background research on the music and poetry of their songs in order to perform them in a stylistically correct and artistically meaningful way, so in theory, the concept of informed performance practice shouldn't be a revelation. However, because Black music tends to be undervalued, labeled as "just" popular music, "just" jazz, and so on, its layers of meaning recede into the background like music on the radio. But that doesn't mean those layers of meaning aren't there, nor is the performer's job any different when approaching repertoire by African American composers, whether it's hip hop or art song.[13] The following quotation from Robert Klotman (president of the Music Educators National Conference from 1978 to 1980) sums up the cultural catch-22 that African American composers face:

> For too long a time, Black composers have been disregarded in our musical society. There are even notorious instances where an established composer who was Black and widely performed had his blackness completely ignored. The past treatment of Black composers has been misleading in terms of the development of our musical culture. Furthermore, it has been damaging by limiting our knowledge regarding this society's musical heritage.[14]

As an example of a song that requires navigating complex racial signifiers, we have chosen "Early in the Mornin'," a selection from David Baker's cycle *The Black Experience*, set to texts by Mari Evans, from her book of poetry entitled *I am a Black Woman*. David Baker (1931–2016) is yet another example of a classically trained African American musician who met resistance in that world and pivoted to jazz for his musical vocation, founding the first jazz studies program in the country in 1968 at Indiana University. According to the Song of America website, "Baker's catalog includes over 2,000 works and is characterized by the fusion of his passions for Western classical music with jazz and other genres. Many of his vocal works choose texts about Black cultural themes and topics."[15] Mari Evans (1923–2017), born in Toledo, Ohio, was a writer associated with the Black Arts Movement, and in her poetry, she celebrated her African American heritage. In an essay entitled "How We Speak," Evans addresses the power of refining the art of listening so that we can hear many complex layers of information, and which we think genuinely describes our task regarding informed performance practice of this repertoire:

> Listening is a special art. It is a fine art developed by practice. One hears the unexpressed as clearly as if it had been verbalized. One hears silence screaming in clarion tones. Ninety decibels. Hears tears, unshed, falling. Hears hunger gnawing at the back of spines; hears aching feet pushed past that one more step. Hears the repressed hurt of incest, hears the anguish of spousal abuse. Hears it all. Clearly, listening is a fine art. It can translate an obscure text into reality that walks, weeps and carries its own odor. *Listening can decode a stranger's eye and hear autobiography (emphasis added)*. Listening can watch a listless babe and understand the absence of future, the improbability, in fact, of possibility. Listening, more often than not, is a crushing experience.[16]

Figure 7.2. "Early in the Mornin'" (Excerpts A and B)

Patterson, Willis C. *Anthology of Art Songs by Black American Composers*. New York: E.B. Marks Music Corp., 1977.

Figure 7.3. "Early in the Mornin'" (Excerpts C and D)
Patterson, Willis C. *Anthology of Art Songs by Black American Composers.* New York: E.B. Marks Music Corp., 1977.

To understand "Early in the Mornin'," the performer and audience alike must engage in the kind of active and layered listening Evans describes in order to perceive the combined messages of the text and music. Mari Evans' poem is a disturbing story of spousal abuse, told in African American Vernacular English, but the music David Baker provides for the telling of this story is a toe-tapping blues number (see Figure 7.2, excerpt A, pickup to m. 5 through m. 8, and excerpt B, mm. 18-25), which seems completely at odds with what is happening in the narrative. However, if you listen carefully, you can hear that Baker frames this narrative with a short, mournful, and dissonant motive (see Figure 7.2, excerpt A, mm. 1-4, and Figure 7.3, excerpt C, mm. 46-50; excerpt D, mm. 90-99) that serves as an introduction, interlude, and postscript, in contrast to the bluesy, "Black-sounding" music for the part of the story that conforms to our racial expectations. In context, this juxtaposition offers a deeper commentary on the emotional toll borne by the characters.

Deep and nuanced listening is crucial to informed performance practice of African American song literature to honor the history and cultural references as well as to acknowledge and move beyond our unconscious value judgments. We have provided much food for thought in this chapter; in the next, we will look at practical ways to develop and teach deep listening skills and implement allyship through activities that build mutual understanding, which can lead to the creation of more representative music ecosystems within the academy.

Notes

1. Reebee Garofalo, "Industrializing African American Popular Music," in *Issues in African American Music: Power, Gender, Race, Representation*, edited by Portia Maultsby and Mellonee Burnim (New York: Routledge, 2017), 90.

2. *Cambridge Advanced Learner's Dictionary & Thesaurus* (Cambridge: Cambridge University Press, 2003).

3. Amélie Lamont, "The Guide to Allyship," accessed January 14, 2023, https://guidetoallyship.com.

4. Sheree Atcheson, "Allyship—The Key to Unlocking the Power of Diversity," *Forbes*, November 30, 2018, https://www.forbes.com/sites/shereeatcheson/2018/11/30/allyship-the-key-to-unlocking-the-power-of-diversity/?sh=1848df4749c6.

5. Atcheson, "Allyship."

6. "Allyship," Wikipedia, accessed January 14, 2023, https://en.wikipedia.org/wiki/Allyship.

7. Caroline Forsey, "What Does Allyship Mean?" *Blog.hubspot.com*, accessed December 16, 2022, http://blog.hubspot.com/marketing/allyship.

8. Atcheson, "Allyship."

9. We are indebted to the work of Emery's research students, Elijah Leer and Jimena Fernández, for their ten-week summer project, in 2021, through the Collaborative Undergraduate Research & Inquiry program at St. Olaf College, Northfield, Minnesota.

10. Banfield, Bill. Cultural Codes: Makings of a Black Music Philosophy: An Interpretive History from Spirituals to Hip Hop. (Lanham, MD: The Rowman & Littlefield Publishing Group, 2010.), ix

11. Patricia Shehan Campbell, David Myers, and Ed Sarath, "Transforming Music Study from Its Foundations: A Manifesto for Progressive Change in the Undergraduate Preparation of Music Majors," *College Music Society Task Force on the Undergraduate Music Major* (2016): 8.

12. Gloria Ladson-Billings, *The Dreamkeepers: Successful Teachers of African American Children*, second edition (San Francisco, CA: Jossey-Bass, 2009), 20.

13. For an interesting discussion of hip hop with its layers of meaning and cultural context, see *Entertaining Race: Performing Blackness in America* by Michael Eric Dyson.

14. Robert H. Klotman, in *The Black Composer Speaks*, edited by David Baker, Lida Belt, and Herman C. Hudson (Metuchen, NJ: Scarecrow Press, 1978), v.

15. Tyrese Byrd, "David Baker," *Song of America*, accessed December 13, 2022, https://songofamerica.net/composer/baker-david-n/.

16. "Mari Evans," *Poetry Foundation*, accessed December 13, 2022, https://www.poetryfoundation.org/poets/mari-evans.

CHAPTER EIGHT

Facilitating Meaningful Conversations and Building Relationships

How to Create Vibrant Music Ecosystems in the Academy

Imagine the feeling of returning from an outstanding conference, where you have met like-minded colleagues, acquired substantive information from expert presenters, and arrived home so excited to begin incorporating changes into your professional practice. We have all been there—ready to make a difference in our communities with our new perspectives and pedagogical approaches. As we move from chapter 7, "Allyship, Permission, and Informed Performance Practice," to chapter 8, our purpose is to allow space to create the "doing" with culturally relevant music, community-building, and self-reflection practices. We will begin by defining an academic music ecosystem and follow with community-building strategies for faculty and administrators—such as deep listening, leading discussions on music and race, facilitating group activities—and propose ways to expand capacity and learning inventory in the classroom. Although building trust through sharing our human experiences is complex, it is a vital first step for sustaining respectful relationships and creating brave spaces to plan culturally relevant programs that serve the students and their audiences.

The idea of "music ecosystems" borrows from the ecological term "ecosystem" in that it encompasses the flow of activity within a given community, identifying collaborative and independent associations and examining how every member is valued and interacts with a particular physical environment. The concept of music ecosystems usually embraces larger goals related to business and production in the music industry, but how can we use this model to help our cause in approaching the music of Black composers within

124 ~ Chapter Eight

the academy? Creating music ecosystems in your institutional community will set the stage (yes, literally) for strategic planning through curriculum discussions, program evaluation, and student learning outcomes.

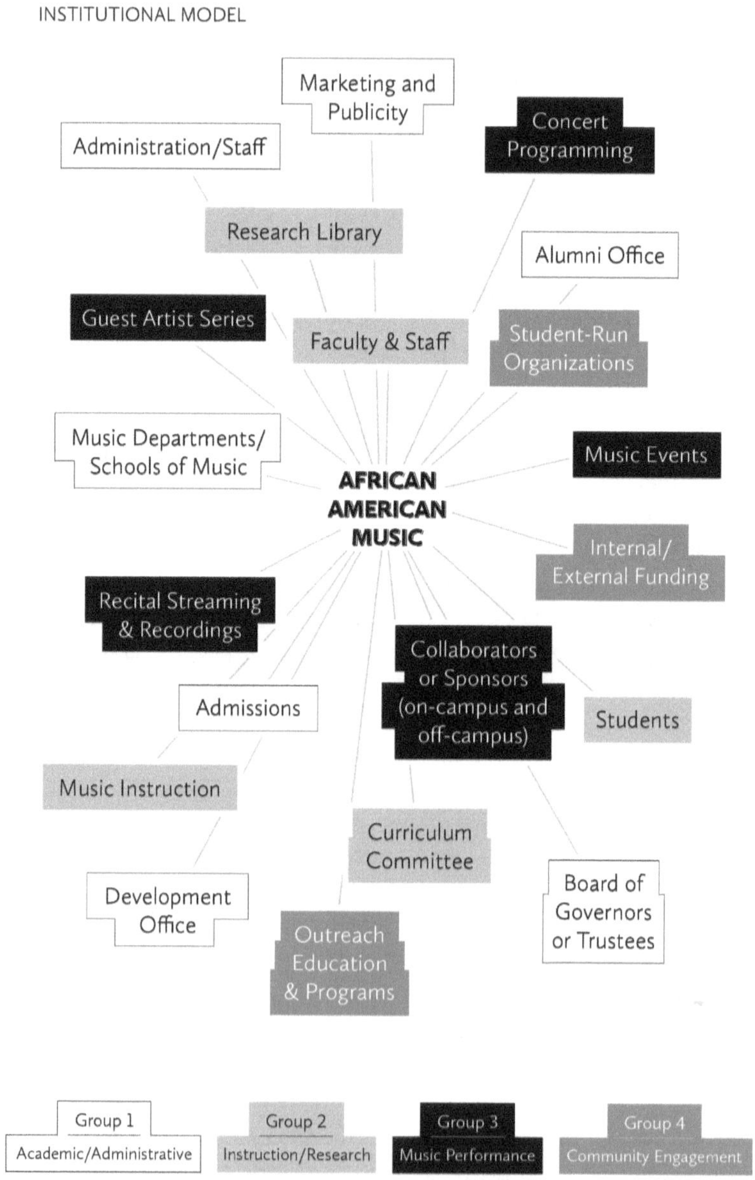

INSTITUTIONAL MODEL

[Diagram centered on **AFRICAN AMERICAN MUSIC** with connected elements: Marketing and Publicity, Administration/Staff, Concert Programming, Research Library, Alumni Office, Guest Artist Series, Faculty & Staff, Student-Run Organizations, Music Departments/Schools of Music, Music Events, Internal/External Funding, Recital Streaming & Recordings, Collaborators or Sponsors (on-campus and off-campus), Students, Admissions, Music Instruction, Curriculum Committee, Development Office, Board of Governors or Trustees, Outreach Education & Programs.]

Group 1 — Academic/Administrative
Group 2 — Instruction/Research
Group 3 — Music Performance
Group 4 — Community Engagement

Figure 8.1. Institutional Music Ecosystem (in the "Academy")
Stephens and Clark, 2023.

Community Building for Administration and Faculty: Walking the Walk

The first step in creating music ecosystems is acknowledging the deliberate exclusion of African Americans from historically White spaces within art or classical music. Historian Kira Thurman states that:

> Silence shrouds many histories of Western art music institutions and their participation in maintaining racial segregation in the nineteenth and twentieth centuries. The profound consequences of the myth of Western art music's color blindness and proclaimed meritocracy, coupled with the historical realities and legacies of racism in the U.S., have created a fraught body of literature on the history of racial minorities at music conservatories.[1]

In another of her articles, Thurman adds that "the recognition of Black composers on any stage puts pressure on institutions to contend with their racist pasts and to imagine a better future. . . . Performing the music of Black composers is not simply or only an opportunity to correct historical wrongs."[2] We have a unique opportunity in the academy at this moment to usher in a paradigm shift that embraces inclusive music curricula and learning experiences. As we know, institutional change is long-term and often challenging for all involved, so let's think outside the box for a minute. What does a music ecosystem look like in a traditional music department, community school, or conservatory setting, and what are some ways for the key players to build trust and communicate effectively while navigating difficult conversations? What follows are some suggestions for intra-group work that faculty and administrators can do to lay the groundwork for meaningful discussion and visioning for developing inclusive curricula.

Developing Deep Listening Skills

Listening is challenging for many of us in a fast-paced, social media–influenced world with tons of information to process. In response, we pressure ourselves to react immediately to complicated or stressful situations, especially concerning uncomfortable topics like race, gender, and microaggressions. Since communication is essential in creating relationships, developing deep listening skills is key to helping groups take time for mindful reflection that serves as a basis for trust and thoughtful, compassionate communication. Even though some readers may be familiar with mindfulness techniques, David Rome shares in the magazine *Mindful* that deep listening practices allow us to listen to ourselves in order to help others, and goes on to say that:

> Deep listening involves listening, from a deep, receptive, and caring place in oneself, to deeper and often subtler levels of meaning and intention in the other person. It is listening that is generous, empathic, supportive, accurate, and trusting. Trust here does not imply agreement but the trust that whatever others say, regardless of how well or poorly it is said, comes from something true in their experience. Deep listening is an ongoing practice of suspending self-oriented, reactive thinking and opening one's awareness to the unknown and unexpected.[3]

Just think about this: How do we usually show up in a given situation? Are we there with the sincere intention to listen before we are motivated to respond? By engaging in cooperative discussions on race and representation in American music, we can identify commonalities as well as differences in shared histories as well as cultural narratives; taking the time to engage in deep listening brings awareness into the space and lays the groundwork for a trustworthy relationship. Once a relationship of trust is established, it is much easier for the group to produce ideas designed to educate and address the systemic underrepresentation of Black music and its composers, songwriters, and artists.

In *The Discussion Book: 50 Great Ways to Get People Talking*, authors Stephen D. Brookfield and Stephen Preskill provide exercises and techniques to help establish effective communication through getting to know each other's stories. Among them is an exercise where two people sit across from each other and take on either the speaker's or the listener's role. The speakers share a professional or personal subject, while listeners focus on what the speaker is sharing without thinking about any immediate response. Listeners may use only questions or affirming words during the conversation. Five to seven minutes are allotted for each speaker, and the listener must summarize what they have heard. (You may also use this exercise as an icebreaker for class discussions or a warm-up for a group discussion.) The following are some examples of questions that can be used to prompt speakers' stories in this listening exercise:

1. What's been occupying your mind lately?
2. What's going on in your work that feels especially challenging right now?
3. If you could be anywhere else right now, where would that be and why?

Other questions that may help listeners draw more from a speaker include "Can you tell me more about that?" "How did that make you feel?" "How did one thing lead to another?" "Why do you think this happened?" and "What did you learn from that experience?"[4] This is a must-have book for developing deep listening skills that lay the groundwork for meaningful and respectful conversations. It is also a great resource for first-time teachers, group facilitators, and anyone interested in community engagement.

Entering Group Discussions
There are some common practices that have proven effective for facilitating respectful yet complex discussions on music and race. One such practice is establishing group goals and norms at the outset through brainstorming and addressing expectations of confidentiality and participation. You may also want to select a timekeeper to ensure equity in "sharing the airtime" and ask participants to respect others' contributions by limiting responses to two to three minutes per person. If you choose to create a learning circle and read a common text, such as *White Fragility* by Robin DiAngelo, *A Little Devil in America: In Praise of Black Performance* by Hanif Abdurraquib, *Dvořák's Prophecy* by Joseph Horowitz, or even an older, foundational work such as *The Souls of Black Folk* by W.E.B. Du Bois, discussion prompts are helpful for facilitators and participants. These prompts provide some structure and accountability for more efficient conversations. When convening a group around a reading assignment, have participants prepare to participate in the discussion by answering some of the following questions ahead of time to engage critically in the discussion. You do not necessarily have to complete all the questions, but at least the first and two other questions which speak to you. You may also add more questions from the group members or choose a scenario on how best to proceed.

1. What is the author's primary objective or argument?
2. How does the reading assignment respond to issues of race and representation, power dynamics, equity, and inclusion or belonging?
3. What are your takeaways? Do you agree or disagree with the author(s)? Any preferences or reactions that you would like to share?
4. Who is the audience, and why do you think the narrative is relevent today?
5. How do the inequities in U.S. power dynamics affect race and ethnicity or privilege in the music industry?
6. Where can we apply concepts and tools of inquiry to analyze race, class, and gender?
7. How are racism, ethnocentrism, power, privilege, and inequality highlighted or explored?

Living Allyship through Action:
Activities for Faculty and Administrators

Institutionally, music schools or departments could begin by conducting surveys and focus groups among faculty and administrators to establish a sense of the climate around diversity, equity, and inclusion (DEI) issues in general as well as specifically gauging emotional responses to reimagining curricula and expanding the canon of American song. Once that data is collected, each institution will be able to tailor a plan of action to its specific needs, because one approach definitely does not work for all. After "taking the temperature" of your community, you could then convene separate meetings with faculty colleagues and administrators—led by a trained, impartial facilitator—to explore common ground as well as differences of opinion, leading to a deeper level of mutual understanding and purpose. Establishing a community of learning after this initial phase of vulnerable communication could be achieved through ongoing dialogue sessions around certain topics, using books, podcasts, or documentaries as a starting point. Individual faculty or administrators can be encouraged to seek out opportunities for DEI professional development (such as attending conferences that will expand their knowledge base and skill set[5]), as well as be rewarded for getting more deeply involved with DEI work across campus. The larger objective of reimagining your curriculum model will be easier to achieve if the individuals in your community have had the opportunity to find their own ways into the conversation.

With all the possible pitfalls and fear of making mistakes that might set off a negative reaction, it is often difficult to decide where to begin in terms of taking action. But keep in mind that, just like when giving emergency first aid, it's better to do something than nothing. Leading from a place of humility, we can acknowledge that we all have more to learn about African American composers and their impact on American music, and give each other grace when we try to address the impact on our art form of the twin elephants in the room: the legacies of chattel slavery and Blackface minstrelsy. Undine Smith-Moore framed the centrality of the problem very well in an interview from 1978 that was published in *The Black Composer Speaks*. She said, "I believe that racism is the chief curse of American society and that there are few problems in American life upon which it does not impinge. The evil effects of racism are as injurious, at least spiritually, to Whites as to Blacks."[6] This thought should put our fears in perspective and empower us to seek all avenues toward a remedy.

Approaches to Student Learning: Classroom Teaching, Student Research, and Performance Projects

Learning Outcomes

Since we have taught courses and presented lecture-recitals and masterclasses on African American art songs and spirituals, we have become aware of the importance of allowing learning outcomes to steer the ways we approach our teaching. Emery recently used them for his undergraduate course in African American song literature at St. Olaf College in the fall of 2022. The following example of the learning outcomes from his syllabus is adaptable to your preference:

- Upon completing the course, students can:
  - Make connections between the reading assignments and the music of African American composers.
  - Describe the relationship between music, race, gender, and privilege.
  - Analyze the song literature through relevant ideas from cultural and historical events to critical race theories.
  - Explore and interpret the repertory of composers of the African diaspora through creative performance and presentation choices.
  - Identify critical resources and notable contributions to African American concert music.

It's much easier to get somewhere when you know your destination, so we would encourage you to contemplate how you can incorporate learning outcomes that address the erasure of African American composers into your syllabi for any related course you teach. Then, when planning the content of your course, you can use a three-pronged approach comprising classroom activities, student research, and performance projects that intentionally center African American contributions for each element.

Classroom Activities

Taking a Learning Inventory

Using a musical quiz as an icebreaker for your voice studio, song literature class, or choral rehearsal classroom is one way to find your students' baseline of awareness and to acknowledge that we are still learning more about the contributions of African Americans to classical music, jazz, and other early genres. The book by Henry V.S. Thomas, *What Do You Know about Blacks in Classical Music* (published in 1989), provides an excellent resource for such an activity. Even though Thomas' book was written in the 1980s and is currently out of print, it provides many essential facts about Blacks in classical music. Thomas begins with an introduction to composers, concert singers, and orchestral conductors and a profile of Black symphony orchestras, dating back to 1897 with the Lyre Club Symphony, and follows with a history of music eras, musical forms, and terms, along with a musical quiz. Here are a few questions from Thomas' book:[7]

- Who wrote the opera *A Christmas Miracle* in 1958?[8]
- What Howard Swanson song was performed by Marian Anderson in 1949 at a Carnegie Hall concert?[9]
- He was the first Black conductor to lead a major symphony orchestra. Name the composer.[10]
- She was one of the first Black Americans to sing opera abroad. In 1927, she made her debut in the title role of Leo Delibes' *Lakme* in Nice, France. Name the opera singer.[11]
- She won critical acclaim for singing both soprano and mezzo-soprano roles in the standard operas. Name the opera singer.[12]

You could revisit this activity over the course of the semester, giving students the opportunity to study the answers to potential questions and win recognition, extra credit, or a special prize for improving their scores when you give a pop quiz. The more we know about Black composers and their music and lived experiences, the better.

Group Text Study

Choose a poem (such as "I, Too" or "Mother to Son" by Langston Hughes), put the students in pairs, and allow them to study its meaning through answering the five Ws: *Who* is the intended audience? *What* is the message? *When* was the poem written, and how does that influence its meaning? *Where* is the original impetus for the poem? *Why* do you think the poet penned these words? Once the students have had an opportunity for one-on-one discussions, you can proceed to a large group discussion in which the class unpacks the meaning of each line, and have them respond to the following questions: Is there a theme or topic that emerges? Of course, both poems focus on Black life in America, but what else do they say to us? Are these poems relevant today regarding race, gender, and equal opportunity? How can we relate them to the given moment and help students understand the responsibility of a performance artist to seek the truth and bring it to the audience?

Comparative Text Study (Songs Side-by-Side)

Pair the students off and have the groups choose two songs by African American composers or songwriters: one classical or spiritual arrangement and one non-classical song. Ask them to write out the entire text or lyrics and discuss the following questions, using the double-column feature in a word processing program to compare the lyrics to both songs.

- What does each song title suggest to you?
- What words strike you as particularly vivid or descriptive?
- What/whose story is centered?
- How does the text make you feel?
- How would you describe the mood (joyful, reflective, anxious, resilient, hopeful, etc.)?
- Who do you imagine is the intended audience? Why do you think the song was written?
- Do you notice any special treatment or effects between the text and music? For example, repeated text, dynamics, word stresses, lyrical phrasing, etc.
- Discuss the mood or energy presented in each song.
- Are there any similarities (structure, message, performance delivery, source material, etc.) between both songs?
- Would you like to add any additional comments?

Once the students have completed this assignment (either in or outside of class time), have them present their comparisons to the rest of the class and lead a large group discussion.

Short Essay Writing

The thirteen-episode series "We, Too, Sing America," a docu-series[13] developed by Aural Compass Projects, centers on a few critical influential Black composers and poets, such as Samuel Coleridge-Taylor, Harry T. Burleigh, Paul Laurence Dunbar, William Grant Still, Margaret Bonds, Florence Price, Adolphus Hailstork, and Undine Smith Moore. Each video is approximately thirty minutes. Have students watch two or more episodes and write a review essay (five hundred to six hundred words maximum) to synthesize a summary of each docu-series video. We will include a link to the "We, Too, Sing America" docu-series in the book's resource section, but you can easily search the internet to find the site. As a follow-up to the activity, you can lead the class in a discussion of the video content.

Group Discussion of Full-Length Films

There are also some wonderful films that explore Black life and music, and watching them together would make an excellent group activity outside of class time that could lead to in-depth discussions during class. Some possibilities include narrative films such as *Raisin in the Sun* (1961), *Ma Rainey's Black Bottom* (2020), and documentary films such as *Marian Anderson: Voice of Freedom* (2021), *Hitsville: The Making of Motown* (2019), *Henry Louis Gates: The Black Church* (2021), *Devil at the Crossroads: A Robert Johnson Story* (2019) on the Delta Blues, *Miles Davis: Birth of the Cool* (2019), *Charlie Pride: It's Just Me* (2019), *Summer of Soul* (2021), and *Amazing Grace* (2018) on the making of Aretha Franklin's epic recording with the same title.

Research Projects

African American Music Timeline

Ask the students to compile a three-page timeline on African American music. It may include multiple genres (classical, jazz, gospel, R&B, neo-soul, hip hop, etc.); think about a fifty/fifty split (50 percent classical music and 50 percent non-classical, or all classical if you prefer. Include historical and political facts (i.e., Great Migration, civil rights, *Brown vs. Board of Education*, Great Depression, World Wars, first Black president of the United States, etc.) to provide the context in which the composers and songwriters created their music. You may reference decades (the 1920s, etc.), a specific year, and date when possible (see the example of a timeline format in chapter 2). When teaching his African American song literature course, Emery found that allowing students to focus on many genres simultaneously engaged the students successfully. Please feel free to adapt the assignment to meet your teaching goals.

Twenty-Song Annotated Playlist (Using PowerPoint or Google Slides)

Another research assignment that allows students to look at Black creators across genres is an annotated playlist assignment. Emery had his students create a playlist on African American composers and songwriters, asking them to choose twenty songs from classical and non-classical genres (again, a roughly fifty/fifty split). He encouraged his students to be creative and choose background themes and layouts that best displayed their work. Then, using only one slide per song, he asked them to include the following information:

- Song Title: Include the music publication date for classical songs and the recording release date for non-classical songs.
- Historical Background: What makes this song important?
- Performing Artist: Short biography (just a few sentences)
- Song Composer/Arranger/Lyricist: Short bio (just a few sentences)
- Embed Video or Audio Performance* (from Naxos, YouTube, Spotify, etc.) to each slide.
- Student Reflection/Comment or Song Analysis: Thirty to fifty words

YouTube/Podcast Deep Dive

Ask the students to explore the resources available on the internet by searching for relevant podcasts or videos and have them choose a few to share with the class. These may include YouTube presentations or documentary series, such as "Sopranos Without Borders," that highlight African American voices. Other options regarding Black cultural and social topics include podcasts by Amazon Music, Spotify, and Apple, such as "The Black Maestro," and several public radio station programs and podcasts, such as "Rhapsody in Black." The radio series "Song of America," by the Hampsong Foundation, founded by the American baritone Thomas Hampson, will offer you a plethora of song information on a curated selection of American music. Encourage students to go beyond the standard Google search when navigating the web by providing them with suggestions for where to find good hyperlinks to reputable sources.

Artistry with an American Accent: Creative Programming Ideas
One of the main pillars of our project is performance, because that's where empathy comes into play, in which the student forms a personal connection to the emotions and characters and history contained in the songs. What follows is a list of possible concert themes that your class can undertake as a group, providing opportunities for creative and organic interweaving of repertoire from composers of all ethnic backgrounds.

- Finding your Roots (aka Henry Louis Gates): each student picks a group of songs that demonstrates their heritage
- Great American poets: the program could include songs by Margaret Bonds + Langston Hughes, Aaron Copland + Emily Dickinson, H.T. Burleigh + Walt Whitman, Florence Price + Paul Laurence Dunbar, Dominic Argento + e.e. cummings, and so on
- Heart of a Woman: *Nightsongs* by Leslie Adams and *Six Poems by Emily Dickinson* by John Duke

- Celebrating the Harlem Renaissance: songs either by Harlem Renaissance composers or set to texts by Harlem Renaissance poets
- Soul music: Songs that speak to your soul across all genres, but beginning and ending with spiritual settings

We think students would say, and many professors would agree, that the recital experience is in need of updating in order to maintain its vitality and relevance in the twenty-first century. In this respect, today's social media and technology environment actually presents great opportunities for revitalizing the song recital. Many performance venues offer in-house technology that makes it possible, for example, to combine performance genres (music, dance, theater, visual artists, spoken word, music and audiovisual technology, projected titles and images, etc.) into a multimedia presentation. Students often have the technical skill with which to create a music series or virtual projects of their own that celebrate Black creators or would relish the planning of a "flash mob" performance in a public space. This repertoire also provides ample opportunities to explore interdisciplinary connections from music to literature to history and the study of American culture, so students in a music class could reach out to students in a history class about the civil rights era, for example, and work together to create a program that demonstrates that time period in song.

Our institutions of higher learning hold so much power to make positive change, but with that power comes the responsibility to act. We hope this chapter has provided a starting point for centering the relevance and necessity of more fully representing the African American voice in our music programs, with contributions by all the members of its music ecosystem. In the next chapter, we will continue to explore the idea of music ecosystems in communities outside the academy, and how the academy can partner with community stakeholders, using music to contribute to the well-being of society.

Notes

1. Kira Thurman, *Singing Like Germans: Black Musicians in the Land of Bach, Beethoven, and Brahms* (Ithaca, NY: Cornell University Press, 2021), 30.

2. Kira Thurman, "When Europe Offered Black Composers an Ear," *New York Times*, August 27, 2021.

3. David Rome, "Healthy Mind, Healthy Life," *Mindful Magazine*, August 26, 2010, https://www.mindful.org/deep-listening/.

4. Stephen D. Brookfield and Stephen Preskill, *The Discussion Book: 50 Great Ways to Get People Talking* (San Francisco: Jossey-Bass, 2016), 111–14.

5. There are many such conferences currently offering this kind of expanded lens for vocal repertoire. The University of Michigan holds an annual summer adult learning conference (the Singing Down the Barriers Institute, Dr. Louise Toppin, director), and the National Association for Teachers of Singing biennial national conference provides many sessions devoted to repertoire by underrepresented or marginalized groups of composers as well as non-classical styles of singing. The African American Art Song Alliance (https://artsongalliance.org/) also holds conferences every five years.

6. *The Black Composer Speaks*, 178–79.

7. Henry V.S. Thomas, *What Do You Know about Blacks in Classical Music* (Baltimore: Gateway Press, Inc., 1989), 167–86.

8. Answer: Mark Fax.

9. Answer: "The Negro Speaks of Rivers."

10. Answer: William Grant Still.

11. Answer: Lillian Evanti.

12. Answer: Shirley Verrett.

13. "We, Too, Sing America: African American Voices of Song," accessed January 14, 2023, https://www.auralcompassprojects.org/we-too-sing-america-series.

CHAPTER NINE

Community Music Engagement, Data Collection, and Audience Development

In this final chapter, we invite readers to amplify efforts through community-based performance projects based on specific demographics, research data, and national trends regarding diversity, equity, inclusion, and belonging initiatives. We will offer readers practical suggestions for engaging community partners by creating meaningful and ongoing relationships with audience members to support thriving music education and community performance projects.

Music performance provides a way to transform lives, expand knowledge, and engage shared humanity through cultural understanding and context. Many students of all ages have benefited from adult and community music education institutions and programs through private music studios, public and independent K–12 schools, colleges, universities, outreach arts programs, and faith-based communities. To illustrate this point, Chesley Talissé writes:

> Community is a fundamental aspect of our experience of music—it tends to unite people, forming bonds that might not exist otherwise. It connects different cultures, promoting diversity and growth. Music encourages creative thinking, discipline, leadership, and problem-solving. And it is a medium for individual and group expression—as Hans Christian Andersen said, "Where words fail, music speaks."[1]

We may ask ourselves a fundamental question, "what is music?" and each of us would define it differently. However, there is no doubt that music is a key to life (no pun intended) and has an enormous impact on communities.

The philosopher Aristotle said, "It is not easy to determine the nature of music or why anyone should have a knowledge of it."[2] However, we believe that music is a transformative, expressive, and communicative tool for communities. Music can be used to share thoughts, memories, and emotions, and honor cultural and religious traditions. Additionally, it may also serve as a social justice vehicle to redress the oppressive structures that foster racism, sexism, ageism, homophobia, ableism, xenophobia, and beyond. As performers from all ethnicities create or seek existing projects to amplify Black voices in the canon, we have a unique vantage point as transformational and inspirational artists to bring social awareness through education and performance toward systemic change. So, how can we think creatively about music genres to reposition the historical importance of Black composers, songwriters, and artists in the center of American music? How can we take the model of community arts education and weave it around our work in telling American stories through the lens of Black history?

Community Arts Education

The National Guild for Community Arts Education, founded in 1937, serves over four hundred organizations and individuals of various artistic disciplines from forty-six states. Many institutional members partner with human services agencies, youth development organizations, public schools, senior centers, and healthcare providers to increase equitable access to arts learning by and for their communities. Their mission is "to ensure all people have opportunities to maximize their creative potential by developing leaders, strengthening organizations, and advocating for community arts education."[3] Since community arts education creates spaces for those who may not have opportunities to pursue formalized music instruction or diverse performance experiences, students can realize their creative potential with artistic providers. The National Guild for Community Arts Education also adds, "People thrive when they participate in community arts education programs that are sustained and responsive to community needs. Arts learning can fuel people's imaginations, build critical knowledge and life skills, promote better health, and generate a sense of shared culture and community belonging."[4] To this point, Emery is a proud product of community arts education from the Community Music Center of Boston when he was in his teens and before he pursued undergraduate and graduate degrees. Emery values the importance of community; he gained experience working with neighborhoods through his employment with the Massachusetts Department of Public Health and his teaching artist residencies with the Boston Lyric Opera, Handel and Haydn

Society, Michigan Philharmonic, Michigan Opera (now the Detroit Opera), and the Arkansas Youth Symphony. Additionally, he worked as a guest clinician with middle and high school students at Mosaic Youth Theatre (Detroit, Michigan), an organizational member of the National Guild for Community Arts Education. Through invitations from colleges and universities and their community partners through our "Singing Down the Barriers" project, we believe in the influence of the wider community when it comes to teaching interdisciplinary tools that support music education, and that the time to act is now. On their website, the National Guild for Community Arts Education describes the urgency of the work:

> As people of color and marginalized communities are disproportionately impacted by the multiple crises of this time, community arts education is more crucial than ever as a vehicle for activism, individual and collective self-expression, and healing.[5]

Among many national examples is the Manhattan School of Music Community Partnerships Program, which serves over thirty-five hundred New Yorkers by performing and bringing music to schools (PreK–grade twelve), senior living residences, hospices, and other community centers throughout New York. Concurrently, several institutions, such as Oberlin College & Conservatory, Eastman School of Music, and the University of North Carolina, have chartered community programs or schools. These institutions offer music education in the community to augment their mission and pedagogical reach in music education. Shain Shapiro, founder and executive director of Center for Music Ecosystems, a global not-for-profit organization that fosters sustainable communities through music, said, "Music can be much more valuable—to all of us—than it is. But we lack a language, lexicon, and framework to explain why music matters outside the sector and how communities can benefit from music no matter where they are."[6] Shapiro's organization focuses on sustainable communities through music ecosystems, including capacity building, networking, business investments (jobs), and lifelong educational opportunities. What is missing when we leave out many Black composers whose music reflects a large majority of American history? Whether establishing short-term or long-term goals, the intentional work to address this question begins with engaging performers, curators, music administrators, artist educators, residents, community businesses, and local leaders.

In their book chapter "Approaching Music Cultures as Ecosystems: A Dynamic Model for Understanding and Supporting Sustainability," the authors Huib Schippers and Catherine Grant present compelling arguments:

When it comes to sustainability, it seems formal education is not necessarily always the ideal. Formal learning (including, but not limited to, that which takes place in institutions) has advantages in terms of stability and prestige. This is one reason musicians and communities may aspire towards it. However, in some cases, formal learning may represent last-resort efforts to maintain some form of transmission for an [underrepresented or non-classical] music genre.[7]

Music education, arts organizations, local businesses, and concert venues are significant partners in creating music ecosystems to thrive in communities. In an illuminating abstract for a book chapter entitled "Community Music Education," the authors Nathan Kruse and Erin Hansen describe their qualitative studies in the activities of diverse and successful community music (CM) models for youth and adults:

> [They] illustrate qualitative studies that exemplify diverse and successful community music (CM) models for youths and adults. [They] illustrate the common musical, social, instructional, and administrative qualities researchers have identified as contributing to the successes of these models and [explore] the growing relevancy of community-based music activities in the United States and [their] relationship to school music education. Categories include band, choral, and orchestral music-making activities; community music schools and summer music programs; cultural connections made through vernacular, folk, and online music experiences; and community music opportunities as social justice.[8]

As a reflective practice, let us examine a potential model for a community-based ecosystem (see Figure 9.1). How could a version of this model function in your community? How could relationships be built between them? Each community is different, so one model will not fit all; however, the suggested ecosystem model can provide a possible road map for building and sustaining a more comprehensive community through the performing arts.

Research and Performance Preparation

As we consider building intentional relationships with community-based organizations, venues, and programs, we must focus on engagement through collaborative research and planning. Researching the demographics, including music venues, civic organizations, businesses, faith-based schools, performing groups, or organizations, is beneficial to building a community profile. According to the U.S. Census Report, the demographics of the population are shifting, with Hispanic or Latino communities (approximately 19

COMMUNITY-BASED MODEL

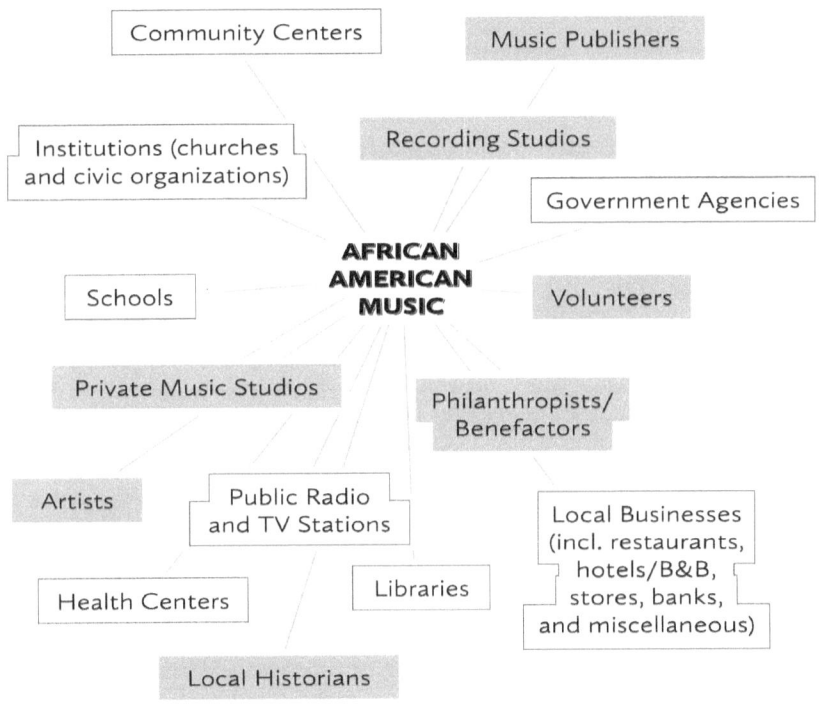

Figure 9.1. Community-Based Music Ecosystem
Stephens and Clark, 2023.

percent) becoming the largest minority group, Black or African American communities making up approximately 14 percent, Asian communities about 6.1 percent, American Indian and Alaska Native around 1.3 percent, and Native Hawaiian and other Pacific Islander comprising under 1 percent. Of the overall population of 333,287,557, approximately 60 percent identify as White (as of July 1, 2022).[9]

Research models may differ depending on your community, from informal to formal; some research methods (surveys, interviews, focus groups, observations, interviews) will be more appropriate than others, depending on your needs. When designing and disseminating surveys about community-based music programming, we recommend identifying people acquainted with research tools, including schools, libraries, local governments, and businesses. Another option is to include a short, written survey at community gatherings to analyze demographics for music programming. If community members prefer using a QR code, create a survey to reach tech-savvy and environmentally conscious individuals. We often recommend hosting community forums or town halls for focus groups and subcommittee meetings around intentional projects on race and music.

In community research, the research hypothesis statement and data questions present an opportunity or address a particular need related to our book topic. In setting up the hypothesis, online research resources are plentiful, and a research specialist in the community would be helpful, but there are a few things to keep in mind. Begin the inquiry with a question. What are you curious about? For example: Do students who study more necessarily get better grades? After selecting a question, conduct preliminary research to answer it with as much pre-existing knowledge as possible. Then, go for a "deeper dive" and look for literature through scholarly sources, reliable online articles or reports, documentaries, or other sources. Evaluating sources and identifying common themes, gaps, or conflicts will help create a research inquiry structure. An example of formulating a hypothesis may look like this: studying more frequently leads to better grades. Then we must refine the hypothesis by being very specific to ensure the best research outcomes. Double-check the research idea and overall plan with someone familiar with the process in the community. Lastly, the hypothesis may be written as 1) an independent statement, 2) a correlation or effects position, or 3) a comparison of two groups.

- *Independent Statement:* If a middle school student begins studying more frequently, they will improve their grades.
- *Correlation or Effects Position:* The number of hours dedicated to studying by middle school students positively affects their class performance.

- *Comparison Model:* Middle school students who study harder will have better testing scores than those who do not study regularly.

Discussing Race-Specific Performance Projects

How do we enter into conversations on race in mixed spaces? Sometimes we assume that everyone is comfortable discussing race, but we know the process can be challenging. Generally, people may be personally challenged and learn a different perspective within a supportive environment for the intentional exchange of ideas. In preparing for these discussions, we want to touch on a few points for facilitators who may need to model or describe how to talk openly yet respectfully if participants have yet to gain first-hand experience with the subject. It is incumbent upon the facilitator to set the tone at the beginning of discussions to ensure that everyone feels valued and safe. We would add that when looking at historical or contemporary readings which use the words "negro," "colored," or the other "n" word, non-Black students may feel uncomfortable or feel strong emotions, not to mention how Black students may feel about the use of these trigger words. White participants may want to refrain from saying these "n" words aloud in public spaces and replace them with "African American" or "Black." Other topics for facilitators to consider before convening a discussion group will vary; however, there must be a concerted effort to determine the comfort level of a group of individuals addressing racism in conversation by discussing preconceptions and social identities while navigating conflicted feelings from past tricky conversations about race. We recommend that each group select a facilitator to regularly take a temperature check with group members to determine their interests and motivations while deciding the structure and community norms (i.e., meeting space and feedback). Reading materials on Black culture may contain African American Vernacular English, which can be troublesome for some people of color to hear from a non-Black member of the group. Following the recent conversations since the murder of George Floyd, many authors and consultants have published works to help steer conversations and reflections when discussing race, and the available resources will no doubt increase. However, we will mention a few resources that are currently available to help address the historical context and preconceptions while introducing terminology, scenarios, exercises, and framing questions for group conversation and reflection. *So You Want to Talk about Race* (Oluo, 2019) and *White Fragility* (DiAngelo, 2018) offer helpful discussion guides for community facilitators and educators; *A Race Is a Nice Thing to Have: A Guide to Being a White Person or Understanding the White Persons in Your Life*

(Helms, 2019) and *Why Are All the Black Kids Sitting Together in the Cafeteria?: And Other Conversations about Race* (Tatum, 2017) will give you ideas, and you may want to consider reading one of these titles for your intentional book group discussions.

Additionally, the National Association of Teachers of Singing (NATS), the world's largest organization of teachers of singing, has created a toolkit of training modules to help members boost diversity and create equitable spaces within the organization. The NATS leadership, with diversity strategist Theresa Ruth Howard and consultant Valarino Boyer, produced training modules (for NATS members). Although the training modules are for NATS members only, the organization created the Inclusion, Diversity, Equity, and Anti-Racism Best Practices Guide,[10] which provides working definitions, guidelines, and helpful ways to think about all types of diversity and how our differences matter, with the purpose of fostering inclusion in the profession.

Setting the Table: Guest Speakers, Teaching Artists, and Cultural Bearers

After gathering research data on the community and analyzing it, we invite you to host guest speakers or visiting artists to your community group, institution, or private studio and even take it further by partnering with several private teachers in the area. This guest visitation will foster connections with local, regional, national, and international experts or cultural bearers. Teachers and students could even spend a significant amount of time hosting artist residencies (short-term or long-term) for lectures, guest performances, interdisciplinary projects, and performances (informal communal singing, formal concerts, and master classes or performance forums). The master class, studio class, or performance forum explores music aesthetics and performance practice by professional clinicians, and we have discovered that this time-honored traditional mode of educational engagement can be a transformative space to engage in complex conversations on race and music. This model provides an opportunity for students to share their thoughts and takeaways regarding their learning inventory and personal challenges. Another option is to commission a composer or songwriter to create a musical work highlighting a specific city or town's history, geographical location, residents, and cultural traditions. This option will involve securing financial support, researching music, planning, and recruiting musicians and other artists (dancers, actors, storytellers, sound engineers, lighting designers, and performance venue owners). Adding community blogs and newsletters will help market and archive partnerships on historical and cultural events on

African American composers, songwriters, and performers. For social media sharing, you can develop themes, culturally relevant events, or fundraising campaigns (i.e., the #Make [Elevate] Black Music Campaign).

Creating Audiences and Equal Opportunities

Audience development involves building meaningful relationships, which goes beyond solely using marketing skills, placing the emphasis on determining the audience's specific needs and wishes. Who are the potential audience members? What do they want to hear? Are there many opportunities to explore Black music and culture across classical and non-classical genres in the community? Is there a possibility to offer blended concerts where jazz, blues, gospel, reggae, R&B, hip hop, classical artists, and more can perform a concert series, individual concerts, or other social events? We believe that audience development involving diverse artistic experiences would be a game-changer for future audiences, especially in classical music, requiring more understanding and training for those unfamiliar with it. Blended genre concerts create a diverse contact list and buy-in for social media and electronic mail lists, such as Mailchimp or email group lists.

When applying for local, state, regional, national or other funding, grant reviewers expect to see collaborations with community partners. Establishing partnerships can be financially beneficial in increasing funding decisions and programmatically attractive to grantors for determining the project's reach among multiple organizations or collaborative artists working toward a unified project. Also, each granting organization, for example, the Southeastern Minnesota Art Council, has a list of review standards which usually include the following elements for applicants to address in their art proposals: 1) artistic merit and quality of the project or program, 2) demand or need for the project or program by the applicant or by the constituents served, and 3) ability of the applicant to accomplish the project or program they describe or the organizational goals as presented.[11] Beyond arts grants, community organizations may raise funds through personal donations, "give as you can" ticket sales, concert subscriptions, or estate planning.

Any opportunities to attend community concerts or non-musical community events will significantly increase your networking opportunities in amplifying Black vocal music. Furthermore, finding adequate and conducive spaces to convene groups is essential. Consider places where all members feel comfortable and equitable means (i.e., transportation and meeting times) are available to get there. Even though there are several spaces available in most communities, such as schools, restaurants, libraries, and civic venues, there is a cross-disciplinary, non-profit organization, Project for Public Spaces, which helps communities reimagine or create public spaces, especially where public spaces in economically challenged communities are not accessible due to poor maintenance or safety concerns. This organization also facilitates partnerships (corporations, foundations, local businesses, and individual donors) to help local partners transform their public spaces. Project for Public Spaces' "groundbreaking placemaking approach helps communities transform their public spaces into vital places that highlight local assets, spur rejuvenation, and serve common needs."[12]

Relationship Building toward Networking

Community partnerships are necessary to create sustainable musical experiences, and community learning at its core is about diverse relationships in tackling a task. As the U.S. economy tightens between arts organizations and higher education due to COVID-19 setbacks, financial recession, or decreasing subscriptions and ticket sales, music organizations and performers must cultivate partnerships with community members to stay viable and survive. Here are a few ideas to consider for networking and building sustainable and vibrant artistic communities.

1. Find affinity groups or create one.
2. Schedule regular (monthly or quarterly) meetings with community arts partners.
3. Identify benefactors or philanthropic organizations.
4. Create a database or spreadsheet for community contacts.
5. Host a community networking or social event.
6. Collaborate on an existing community event—support for a particular cause.

Scenario Exercise: Using a community-based ecosystem model explicitly designed for a specific city or town, how would the community approach commissioning a musical work by an established or emerging African American composer for an event or celebration? How would that process unfold in your community?

In terms of classical music, in 1936, Alain Locke echoed Dvořák's sentiment when he wrote: "The Negro has been the main source of America's popular music, and promises, as we shall see, to become one of the main sources of America's serious or classical music, at least that part which strives to be natively American and not derivative of European types of music."[13] Considering Locke's sentiments, we could introduce an ice-breaker for group meetings and discussions to identify the need for community engagement regarding centering the study and performance of African American song literature. Invite each group member to list at least five African American composers and share their responses with the group. Then analyze the responses to see if you notice any similarities or patterns. If the group decides to go further, ask members to list how many White composers they know. Is it easier to name White composers than Black composers? Would you suppose it is easier to list the White composers since they are significant subjects studied in school? Emery discovered that the Smithsonian's National Museum of African American History and Culture in Washington, DC, produced a bookmark featuring Black trailblazers, such as agricultural scientist, innovator, educator, and artist (poet and painter) George Washington Carver (1864–1943); entrepreneur, philanthropist, and social activist Madam C.J. Walker (1867–1919); and orator, abolitionist, editor, and statesman Frederick Douglass (1818–1895). Each bookmark contains a photo on one side with a short bio on the other. Wouldn't it be a great idea to sponsor a community activity or even a contest to create bookmarks to learn about African American composers? Although this activity will involve research and purchasing art materials for the paper bookmark, it would be an innovative way to unite community members. These bookmarks could be collected and distributed to schools, local libraries, businesses, and retirement communities as a community event. Even though this activity will involve research, the result would be a creative way to learn about influential African American composers and musicians.

Let us try another "getting to know you" exercise for group sharing opportunities. Invite group members to share in a performance event to celebrate music (any genre) and spoken word by African Americans—what would you share with them? Emery had the opportunity to engage undergraduate students in this exercise during a general education course where student performers sang "Night" (Leslie Adams), "Deep River" (Moses Hogan), "Freight Train (Elizabeth Cotten), "Give Me One Reason" (Tracy Chapman), "Were I a Star" (H.T. Burleigh), "Winter Moon" (Margaret Bonds), "Don't Touch My Hair" (Solange), and "Your Daddy's Son" from *Ragtime*. For students who were uncomfortable singing, they offered spoken word performances of the following readings: "Human Family" (Maya Angelou), "Hanging Fire" (Audre Lorde), "If We Must Die" (Claude McKay), "Booker T. and W.E.B." (Dudley Randall), "Caged Bird" and "Phenomenal Woman" (Maya Angelou), and "Father Son and Holy Ghost" (Audre Lorde).

In developing your community ecosystem, determine your goals or reexamine them based on your community-based music ecosystem and see if they need to be expanded to explore meaningful conversations that inspire change, especially in engaging students in the twenty-first century, through the following questions: "Who benefits when we perform African-American music?" "What types of stories are being told?" "How do I connect to these Black song narratives?" "How can we embrace these lived experiences with care and respect?" and finally, "Should we expect reparations that include centering Black music holistically in the canon?" Could a concert or music series involve a dance studio, company, or local visual artist who would showcase their work during a concert in some form, such as building stage sets or hosting an art show? Moreover, improvisation circles (drumming, singing, miming) can be interactive ways to build relationships while having fun and discovering individual talents without a formalized event or performance.

Think about reparations that would serve Black concert music when researching and choosing works by African American composers that are not regularly performed but need more significant exposure. Even though we have emerging composers, consider conducting research on works not currently in the traditional canon (or that are less well known) and offering the community a new experience by presenting an underrepresented work, such as *The Ballad of the Brown King* (dedicated to Martin Luther King) with text by Langston Hughes and music by Margaret Bonds; *Son of Man* (1946) by Hall Johnson; *Cantata for baritone, narrator, chorus, and orchestra* (1948) by Julia Perry; and new works including a commissioned choral work, *Dreamland: Tulsa, 1921* by the Turtle Creek Chorale (2022) and the *Requiem for the Enslaved* (2021) by Carlos Simon, for spoken word, instrumental ensemble, and piano, to name a few.

Finding prospective scores to consider for music projects may take a while. From researching libraries, composer archives, to online search engines,[14] we encourage readers to unearth musical gems by contacting composer estates, music scholars, or research librarians. What would be a potential project? How do we further amplify African American composers? Why do you think African American classical composers are underrepresented in music education? Does one feel that non-classical music is valued more than classical compositions?

Attending Concerts in the Community

Music-making can be inspiring and, in some cases, a celebratory or healing experience where we learn about ourselves and others in new, respectful ways. In centering efforts for diversity, equity, inclusion, and belonging, we realize that the art of music breaks down barriers, and we learn about our shared humanity in the world. Every time we attend a concert, we experience a community of artists who usually bring a well-rehearsed traditional and contemporary works program. Even though it sounds cliché, music-making creates opportunities to express, collaborate, and communicate with others. Music performance is a creative social endeavor and invites audience participation through an emotional and aesthetic exchange between the performer and the audience. Music perception is social, too: audiences recognize social relationships and communicative behavior between members of a performing ensemble,[15] and they infer human agency when hearing music—even without visual confirmation of a performer[16]—making sounded performances a means of interpersonal communication.[17]

Final Thoughts

In closing, our project has been focused on finding ways to engage students and vocal colleagues with the context and embodiment of music by African Americans while amplifying efforts to learn from mistakes in history, such as omission, erasure, and racial inequality. We can become more unified in our shared American history by telling our stories through song, and performers can lead by example when they have built music ecosystems that support intentional music making with permission and respect. We leave your community with this final quote to inspire the journey forward by American guitarist, singer, and songwriter Jimi Hendrix: "If there is something to be changed in this world, then it can only happen through music." We hope you have gathered historical context, ideas, resources, tools, and inspiration to create or strengthen current music ecosystems on the community level. No ethnic group alone can overcome all the barriers we have discussed. However, we are passionate about "singing them down" by creating inclusive cultural spaces where Black voices are amplified, valued, and respected through equal opportunities in the industry. By encouraging creative community-based music ecosystems, we enable individual performers, music groups, whether classical or non-classical, to prepare innovative artistic projects on Black music for community or public school audiences and to think outside of the box to become musical ambassadors.

Notes

1. Chesley Talissé, "Building a Sense of Community with Music," June 20, 2018, https://www.edutopia.org/article/building-sense-community-music.

2. Anselm H. Amadio, "Aristotle," *Encyclopedia Britannica*, accessed November 9, 2022, https://www.britannica.com/biography/Aristotle.

3. The National Guild for Community Arts Education, accessed January 14, 2023, https://nationalguild.org/about/about-the-guild.

4. The National Guild for Community Arts Education, accessed January 14, 2023, https://nationalguild.org/about/about-the-guild.

5. The National Guild for Community Arts Education, accessed January 14, 2023, https://nationalguild.org/about/about-the-guild.

6. Shain Shapiro, "Why We Need to Think about Music Ecosystems to Grow the Industry and Sector," *Musically.com*, February 15, 2022, https://musically.com/2022/02/15/why-we-need-to-think-about-music-ecosystems-to-grow-the-industry-and-sector-guest-column/.

7. Huib Schippers and Catherine Grant, "Approaching Music Cultures as Ecosystems: A Dynamic Model for Understanding and Supporting Sustainability," in *Sustainable Futures for Music Cultures: An Ecological Perspective*, edited by Huib Schippers and Catherine Grant (New York: Oxford Academic, 2016).

8. Nathan B. Kruse and Erin M. Hansen, "Community Music Education," in *The Oxford Handbook of Qualitative Research in American Music Education*, edited by Colleen M. Conway, Oxford Academic (June 2, 2014), https://doi.org/10.1093/oxfordhb/9780199844272.013.026.

9. U.S. Census Data, accessed January 5, 2023, https://www.census.gov/quickfacts/fact/table/US/PST045221.

10. I.D.E.A. Toolkit, accessed January 14, 2023, https://www.nats.org/IDEA_Toolkit.html.

11. Southeastern Minnesota Arts Council, http://semac.org/resources/glossary.php#4.

12. Project for Public Spaces, https://www.pps.org/about.

13. Earl Ofari Hutchinson, *It's Our Music Too: The Black Experience in Classical Music* (Los Angeles, CA: Middle Passages Press, 2016), 95.

14. Such as Dr. Louise Toppin's African Diaspora Music Project, https://africandiasporamusicproject.org/.

15. Moran, N., Hadley, L. V., Bader, M., and Keller, P. E. (2015). Perception of 'back-channeling' nonverbal feedback in musical duo improvisation. PLoS ONE 10:e0130070. doi: 10.1371/journal.pone.0130070; Aucouturier, J. J., and Canonne, C. (2017). Musical friends and foes: The social cognition of affiliation and control in improvised interactions. Cognition 161, 94–108. doi: 10.1016/j.cognition.2017.01.019.

16. Olsen, K. N., and Dean, R. T. (2016). Does perceived exertion influence perceived affect in response to music? Investigating the "FEELA" hypothesis. Psychomusicol. Music Mind Brain 26, 257 -269. doi: 10.1037/pmu0000140.

17. Laura Bishop, "Collaborative Musical Creativity: How Ensembles Coordinate Spontaneity," *PubMed.gov*, July 24, 2018, doi: 10.3389/fpsyg.2018.01285.

Selected Bibliography and Resources

Foundational Publications

Aberjhani and Sandra L. West. *The Encyclopedia of the Harlem Renaissance*. New York: Checkmark Books, 2003.

Abromeit, Kathleen A. *Spirituals: A Multidisciplinary Bibliography for Research and Performance*. Middleton, WI: Co-published by Music Library Association and A-R Editions, Inc., 2015.

Burnim, Mellonee, and Portia Maultsby, eds. *African American Music: An Introduction*. Second edition. New York and London: Routledge (Taylor & Francis Group), 2015.

Caldwell, Hansonia. *African American Music: A Chronology 1619-1995*. Los Angeles, CA: Ikoro Communications, n.d.

Cone, James H. *A Black Theology of Liberation*. New York: Lippincott, 1970.

Crawford, Richard. *America's Musical Life: A History*. New York: Norton, 2001.

Floyd, Samuel A., ed. *International Dictionary of Black Composers*. Chicago: Fitzroy Dearborn Publishers, 1999.

Floyd, Samuel A. *The Power of Black Music: Interpreting Its History from Africa to the United States*. New York: Oxford University Press, 1995.

Jones, Randye. *So You Want to Sing Spirituals: a Guide for Performers*. Lanham: Rowman & Littlefield, 2019.

Locke, Alain. *The Negro and His Music*. Washington, DC: The Associates in Negro Folk Education, 1936.

Maultsby, Portia K., and Mellonee V. Burnim. *Issues in African American Music: Power, Gender, Race, Representation*. Edited by Portia K. Maultsby and Mellonee V. Burnim. New York, NY: Routledge, 2017.

152 ～ Selected Bibliography and Resources

Price, Emmett George, Tammy L. Kernodle, and Horace J. Maxile. *Encyclopedia of African American Music*. Santa Barbara, CA: ABC-CLIO, 2011.
Southern, Eileen. *The Music of Black Americans: A History*. Third edition. New York: Norton, 1997.
Wintz, Cary and Paul Finkelman, eds. *Encyclopedia of the Harlem Renaissance*. New York: Routledge, n.d.

Where to Go for More Information; Take a Deeper Dive into a Specific Area

Spirituals
Allison, Roland L. "Classification of the Vocal Works of Harry T. Burleigh (1866-1949) and Some Suggestions for their Use in Teaching Diction in Singing." Ph.D. dissertation, Indiana University, 1965.
Barber, Felicia Raphael Marie, and André J. Thomas. *A New Perspective for the Use of Dialect in African American Spirituals: History, Context, and Linguistics*. Lanham: Lexington Books, 2021.
Bibbs, Susheel. *The Art of the Spiritual: Enhancing Performance of the Concert Spiritual*. Sacramento, CA: Daya Kay Communications, Inc., 2016.
Boatner, Edward. *The Story of the Spirituals: Thirty Spirituals and Their Origins*. Melville, NY: Belwin Mills, 1973.
Cruz, Jon. *Culture on the Margins: The Black Spiritual and the Rise of American Cultural Interpretation*. Princeton: Princeton University Press, 1999.
Graham, Sandra J. *Spirituals and the Birth of a Black Entertainment Industry*. Urbana: University of Illinois Press, 2018.
Guenther, Eileen Morris. *In Their Own Words: Slave Life and the Power of Spirituals*. Saint Louis, MO: MorningStar Music Publishers, 2016.
Lovell, John. *Black Song: The Forge and the Flame; the Story of How the Afro-American Spiritual Was Hammered Out*. New York: Macmillan, 1972.
Simpson, Eugene T. *The Hall Johnson Concert Spirituals*. West Conshohocken, PA: Infinity Publishing, 2015.
Thomas, André J., and Anton Armstrong. *Way over in Beulah Lan': Understanding and Performing the Negro Spiritual*. Dayton, OH: Heritage Music Press, 2007.
Thurman, Howard. *Deep River and the Negro Spirituals Speak of Life and Death*. Richmond, IN: United Friends Press, 1975.

Popular Music
Brooks, Tim. *Lost Sounds: Blacks and the Birth of the Recording Industry, 1890-1919*. Urbana: University of Illinois Press, 2005.

Hamm, Charles. *Yesterdays: Popular Song in America*. New York: W.W. Norton & Company, 1979.
Higgins, Nathan. *Harlem Renaissance*. Oxford: Oxford University, 1971.
Jasen, David, and Gene Jones. *Spreadin' Rhythm Around: Black Popular Songwriters, 1880-1930*. Schirmer Trade Books, n.d.
Spencer, Jon Michael. *The New Negroes and Their Music: The Success of the Harlem Renaissance*. First edition. Knoxville: The University of Tennessee Press, 1997.

Concert Music

André, Naomi Adele, Karen M. Bryan, Eric Saylor, and Karen M. Bryan. *Blackness in Opera*. Urbana: University of Illinois Press, 2013.
Baker, David, Lida Belt Baker, and Herman C. Hudson. *The Black Composer Speaks*. Metuchen, NJ: Scarecrow Press, 1978.
Banfield, William. *Landscapes in Color: Conversations with Black American Composers*. Metuchen, NJ: Scarecrow Press, Inc., 1998.
Floyd, Samuel A. *Black Music in the Harlem Renaissance: A Collection of Essays*. New York: Greenwood Press, 1990.
Floyd, Samuel A. *The Power of Black Music: Interpreting Its History from Africa to the United States*. New York: Oxford University Press, 1995.
Green, Mildred Denby. *Black Women Composers: A Genesis*. Boston, MA: Twayne Publishers, 1983.
Holly, Ellistine Perkins. *Biographies of Black Composers and Songwriters: A Supplementary Textbook*. Dubuque, IA: Wm. C. Brown Publishers, 1990.
Horowitz, Joseph. *Dvořák's Prophecy: and the Vexed Fate of Black Classical Music*. First edition. New York: W. W. Norton & Company, Inc., 2022.
Krehbiel, Henry E. *Afro-American Folksongs: A Study in Racial and National Music*. New York: Frederick Ungar Publishing Co., 1962.
Price, Emmett George, Tammy L. Kernodle, and Horace J. Maxile. *Encyclopedia of African American Music*. Santa Barbara, CA: ABC-CLIO, 2011.
Roach, Hildred. *Black American Music: Past and Present*. Second edition. Malabar, FL: Krieger Pub. Co., 1992.
Stewart, Earl L. *African American Music: An Introduction*. New York: Schirmer Books, 1998.
Thurman, Kira. *Singing Like Germans: Black Musicians in the Land of Bach, Beethoven, and Brahms*. Ithaca, NY: Cornell University Press, 2021.
Walker-Hill, Helen. *From Spirituals to Symphonies: African American Women Composers and their Music*. New York: Greenwood Publishing, 2002.
———. *Music by Black Women Composers: A Bibliography of Available Scores*. Chicago: Center for Black Music Research, 1995.

Selected Performer Autobiographies and Biographies

- *Bricktop* (aka Ada Smith) by Bricktop with James Haskins | 1983
- *His Eye Is on the Sparrow: An Autobiography* by Ethel Waters | 1992
- *Ethel Waters: Stormy Weather* by Stephen Bourne | 2007
- *Harry T. Burleigh: From Spiritual to the Harlem Renaissance* by Jean Snyder | 2016
- *Here I Stand* by Paul Robeson | 1998
- *I Never Walked Alone: The Autobiography of an American Singer* by Shirley Verrett and Christopher Brooks | 2003
- *In One Lifetime: A Biography of William Grant Still* by Verna Arvey | 1989
- *James P. Johnson: A Case of Mistaken Identity* by Scott Brown | 1986
- *Jazz Cleopatra: Josephine Baker in Her Time* by Phyllis Rose | 1989
- *Josephine Baker: The Hungry Heart* by Jean-Claude Baker and Chris Chase | 2001
- *Josephine Baker's Last Dance* by Sherry Jones | 2018
- *King of Ragtime: Scott Joplin and His Era* by Edward Berlin | 2016
- *Mahalia Jackson and the Black Gospel Field* by Mark Burford | 2019
- *Roland Hayes: The Legacy of an American Tenor* by Christopher Brooks and Robert Sims | 2014
- *Soul on Soul: The Life and Music of Mary Lou Williams* | 2020
- *Songs and Spirituals: The Life and Music of Jacqueline Hairston* by Phillip Harris | 2020
- *The Heart of a Woman: The Life and Music of Florence B. Price* by Rae Linda Brown | 2020
- *The Undiscovered Paul Robeson: An Artist's Journey, 1898-1939* by Paul Robeson | 2001
- *The Undiscovered Paul Robeson: Quest for Freedom* by Paul Robeson | 2010
- *Father of the Blues: An Autobiography* by W.C. Handy | 1991
- *W.C. Handy: The Life and Times of the Man Who Made the Blues* by David Robertson | 2009
- *William Grant Still (American Composers)* by Catherine Smith | 2008

Articles

Anderson, Colin L. "Segregation, Popular Culture, and the Southern Pastoral: The Spatial and Racial Politics of American Sheet Music, 1870–1900." *The Journal of Southern History* 85, no. 3 (2019): 577–610.

Breedlove, Thomas. "To Sing Against Singing: Constraint and Liberation in the Spirituals of Roland Hayes." *Political Theology: The Journal of Christian Socialism* 22, no. 6 (2021): 475–92.

Giles, Mark S. "Howard Thurman, Black Spirituality, and Critical Race Theory in Higher Education." *The Journal of Negro Education* 79, no. 3 (Summer, 2010): 354–65, 438.

Hogges, Genithia Lilia. "Canonization Reconstructed Inclusion and Exclusion in Nineteenth-Century African-American Periodicals with an Ear to the Music of African Americans." *American Periodicals* 12 (2002): 152–62.

Lawrence-McIntyre, Charshee Charlotte. "The Double Meanings of the Spirituals." *Journal of Black Studies* 17 (June 1987): 397–401.

Pedagogy

Dunn-Powell, Rosephanye. "The African-American Spiritual: Preparation and Performance Considerations." *Journal of Singing* 61, no. 5 (May/June 2005): 469–75.

Ivey, Donald. "Willis Patterson's 'Anthology of Art Songs by Black American Composers.'" *Black Music Research Journal* 2 (1981-1982): 106–26.

Patterson, Willis. "The African-American Art Song: A Musical Means for Special Teaching and Learning." *Black Music Journal* 16, no. 2 (Autumn 1996): 303–10.

Plant, Lourin. "Singing African-American Spirituals: A Reflection on Racial Barriers in Classical Music." *Journal of Singing* 60, no. 5 (May/July 2005): 451–68.

Steinhaus-Jordan, Barbara. "Black Spiritual Art Song: Interpretive Guidelines for Studio Teachers." *Journal of Singing* 61, no. 5 (May/June 2005): 477–85.

Stephens, Emery, and Caroline Helton. "Diversifying the Playing Field: Solo Performance of African American Spirituals and Art Songs by Voice Students from all Racial Backgrounds." *Journal of Singing* 70, no. 2 (Nov. 2013): 165–71.

Taylor, Darryl. "The Importance of Studying African-American Art Song." *Journal of Singing* 54, no. 3 (1998): 9–16.

Warfield, William. "The Keynote Address." *The Black Perspective in Music* 14, no. 1 (1986): 7–12.

Wilson, Olly. "Black Music as an Art Form." *Black Music Research Journal* 3 (1983): 1–22.

Docuseries

"We, Too, Sing America"
https://www.auralcompassprojects.org/we-too-sing-america-series

Note

1. Please note that this appendix is only a partial list of all the excellent resources that are available. The purpose of this curated bibliography is to give readers a starting point for building their libraries.

Selected Song Anthologies and Collections

Bonds, Margaret. *In His Hand: Seven Spirituals for Voice and Piano.* King of Prussia, PA: Theodore Presser, 2010.

Brown, Jr., Uzee. *O Redeemed!: A Set of African–American Spirituals for Medium–Low or Medium-High Voice and Piano.* Dayton, OH: R. Dean Publishing, 1994.

Bullock, Kathy W., and Donna M. Cox, eds. *Art Songs and Spirituals by Contemporary African American Composers.* Xenia, OH: Personal Best Ministries, 2011.

Burleigh, Harry T. *Album of Negro Spirituals, Arranged for Solo Voice.* Melville, NY: Belwin Mills Publishing Corp., 1917.

Hairston, Jacqueline B., and Phillip Harris. *Songs and Spirituals.* Volume I. Fayetteville, AR: Classical Vocal Reprints, 2019.

Hayes, Roland. *My Favorite Spirituals: Thirty Songs for Voice and Piano.* Mineola, NY: Dover Publications, Inc., 2001.

Headlee, Celeste Anne, ed. *William Grant Still: An Art Song Collection.* Flagstaff, AZ: The Master-Player Library (William Grant Still Music), 2000.

Heard, Richard. *44 Art Songs and Spirituals by Florence B. Price.* Fayetteville, AR: ClarNan Editions, 2015.

Hogan, Moses. *The Deep River Collection: Ten Spirituals for Solo Voice & Piano.* Milwaukee: Hal Leonard Publishing Corp., 2000.

Johnson, Hall. *The Hall Johnson Collection.* Chicago: Carl Fischer, 2003.

———. *Thirty Spirituals.* New York: G. Schirmer, 1949.

Johnson, J. Rosamond. *Album of Negro Spirituals* (newly adapted and arranged). Milwaukee: Hal Leonard Publishing Group, 1984.

Johnson, James Weldon, and J. Rosamond Johnson. *The Books of American Negro Spirituals.* New York: Da Capo Press, 1973.

Lloyd, Jr., Charles. *The Spiritual Art Song Collection.* Van Nuys, CA: Alfred Publishing, 2000.

McLin, Lena J. *Songs for Voice & Piano* (Medium High Voice). San Diego, CA: Kjos Music, 2003.

Okpebholo, Shawn E. *The Shawn E. Okpebholo Collection of Negro Spirituals.* Wheaton, IL: Yellow Einstein Press, 2013.

———. *The Shawn E. Okpebholo Collection of Reimagined Negro Spirituals and Folk Hymns.* Volume 2. Wheaton, IL: Yellow Einstein Press, 2022.

Patterson, Willis C., ed. *Anthology of Art Songs by Black American Composers.* First edition. New York: Edward B. Marks Music Company, 1977.

———. *The Second Anthology of Art Songs by African American Composers.* Ann Arbor: Videmus, 2002.

Patterson, Willis C. *The New Negro Spiritual Collection.* Ann Arbor: Videmus, 2002.

Price, Florence B. Price. *44 Art Songs and Spirituals,* edited by Richard Heard. Fayetteville, AR: ClarNan Editions, 2015.

Ragland, Dave. *Spirituals & Art Songs.* Nashville, TN: Dave Ragland, 2017. (high/low voice editions)

Sneed, Damien. *Spiritual Sketches.* New York: Lechateau Arts Publishers, 2013.

Simmons, Margaret R., Jeanine Wagner, and Jeanine Wagner. *A New Anthology of Art Songs by African American Composers.* Carbondale, IL: Southern Illinois University Press, 2004.

Soll, Beverly, ed. *William Grant Still: Arias, Duets, and Scenes from the Operas.* Flagstaff, AZ: William Grant Still Music, 1998.

Still, William Grant. *Twelve Negro Spirituals. Arranged for Voice(s) and Piano.* Edited by Wellington Adams. New York: Handy Bros. Music Co., 2008.

Taylor, Vivian, ed. *Art Songs and Spirituals by African-American Women Composers.* Bryn Mawr, PA: Hildegard Publishing Company, 1995.

Toppin, Louise, Scott Piper, eds. *An Anthology of African and African Diaspora Songs.* Fayetteville, AR: Classical Vocal Reprints, 2021.

From the Videmus Art Song Series.

Toppin, Louise, ed. *Rediscovering Margaret Bonds: Art Songs, Spirituals, Musical Theater and Popular Songs.* Fayetteville, AR: Classical Vocal Reprints, 2021.

Toppin, Louise, ed. *Art Songs with Sacred Texts for High Voice by Adolphus Hailstork.* Fayetteville, AR: Classical Vocal Reprints, 2020.

Toppin, Louise, ed. *Chamber Music: Songs for Soprano and Strings by Adolphus Hailstork.* Fayetteville, AR: Classical Vocal Reprints, 2020.

Toppin, Louise, ed. *Songs for Soprano and Harp by Adolphus Hailstork.* Fayetteville, AR: Classical Vocal Reprints, 2020.

Toppin, Louise, ed. *Deux Chansons for Soprano, Bb Clarinet and Piano by Adolphus Hailstork.* Fayetteville, AR: Classical Vocal Reprints, 2020.

Toppin, Louise, ed. *Art Songs for High Voice by Adolphus Hailstork.* Fayetteville, AR: Classical Vocal Reprints, 2020.

Glossary

AAVE: African American Vernacular English.
Academy: An institution of learning or teaching.
Allyship: Any individuals or groups supporting marginalized people or social causes.
Antebellum: This term refers to the pre–Civil War (1861–1865) period of U.S. history.
Apollo Theatre: A central theater in Harlem, New York, built in 1913 for African American popular music.
Bebop: A modern, early to mid-1940s jazz style (also known as "bop").
Blackface minstrelsy: A popular nineteenth-century entertainment featuring White performers first and then Black performers darkening their faces with black stage make up while portraying stereotypical and often disrespectful depictions of African Americans.
Black Intelligentsia: Middle- and upper-class, educated, African American citizens in the United States in the late nineteenth century.
Black Swan Records: A widely distributed Black record label founded by Harry Pace, in 1921, in Harlem, New York, to support American jazz and blues artists.
Blues: The popular form of secular folk music that emerged in the south around the 1860s by African Americans.
Canon: A collection or core set of pieces known and performed often, especially in the history of classical music.

Civil Rights Movement: African Americans' social and political struggle in the 1950s and 1960s for racial equality and social justice.

Clef Club: The concert venue and social club, incorporated by James Reese Europe in 1910, for African American musicians in Harlem; this organization began the first African American orchestra in the country, named the Clef Club Orchestra.

Community-based: An activity or project that is organized and presented locally.

Cultural appropriation: The disrespectful taking of cultural aesthetics or material from another culture or identity without cultural context, consent, permission, or relationship; the use is solely for personal interest or gain

DEIB: Diversity, equity, inclusion, and belonging.

Emancipation: An edict or official political document by President Abraham Lincoln (1809–1865) on January 1, 1863, to signify the freeing of the enslaved persons in Confederate states still in rebellion from the Civil War.

Eurocentric: Focuses on the importance of the dominance of European culture.

Gilded Age: An economic boom resulting from exponential growth in immigration and a concentration of wealth at the top socioeconomic echelon from 1877 to c. 1900, especially in the northern and western United States; this period is known for the philanthropy of super-wealthy individuals, but also for the extremes of capitalism that produced such wealth, along with classism and often corruption, where businessmen and politicians could be described as living "fat" and on the backs of the working class.

Great Migration: The most significant relocation of African Americans in U.S. history from the southern states to the northern, midwestern, and western states from the 1910s to 1970s.

Harlem Renaissance: An influential period of intellectual, artistic, and social development centered in Harlem, New York, beginning in the 1920s.

HBCUs: Historically Black colleges and universities.

HUAC: The House on Un-American Activities Committee.

Jazz: An American music genre of the late nineteenth and early twentieth centuries with distinct roots from blues and ragtime.

Jim Crow: The term originated with a stock character from Blackface minstrelsy, but was later used to describe laws designed to subjugate African Americans and segregate them from the White population in the Southern United States.

Met: Metropolitan Opera.

Music ecosystem: A term that applies to the multiplicitous conditions, businesses, institutions, and social groups responsible for supporting thriving artistic, cultural, and music education programs in a given community.

New Negro Movement: Another historical name for the Harlem Renaissance, inspired by the 1925 anthology, *The New Negro*, edited by Alain Locke (1885–1954).

NAACP: National Association for the Advancement of Colored People

NANM: National Association of Negro Musicians.

NATS: National Association of Teachers of Singing.

Negro spirituals: The historical term for the religious folk songs created by African Americans during enslavement in the United States.

Performance practice: A term used to describe how music should be accurately and respectfully presented.

Ragtime: A popularized musical style for piano during the early twentieth century with a syncopated melody and rhythmically firm bass accompaniment.

Reconstruction: The period of transition and legal, political, and social restoration from 1865–1877 following the American Civil War.

Rhythm and blues: A popular music genre that mixed jazz, blues, and Black gospel idioms, originating in the African American community in the 1940s.

Rock and roll: A 1950s dance-inspired music genre characterized by the Black gospel and pop traditions and popularized by Black and White listeners.

Swing: A style of jazz that developed in the 1930s and became popular among big bands and swing dancers.

SMTD: School of Music, Theatre & Dance, the University of Michigan.

Tin Pan Alley: A collection of New York–based publishers and songwriters who produced commercial songs (i.e., vaudeville, ballads, dance music) in the late nineteenth and early twentieth centuries.

PWI: Predominately white institutions.

Talented Tenth: A term coined by W.E.B. Du Bois in a 1903 essay to prompt African American men to use their education and leadership to benefit the Black community in the early twentieth century.

Index

Aaron Copland Award, 113
Abdurraquib, Hanif, 127
abolitionism, 9–10
action plans, 111
Adams, Leslie, 134
administration: activities for, 128; community-building for, 125–28
Aeolian, 21
"The African-American Art Song" (Patterson), 48
African American Art Song Alliance, xxvi, 135n5
African American composers, xviii; absence of, from American song anthologies, xxiii; anthologies of, xxvii; contributions of, xxvii; entry points for centering of, 71–73; recognition of, 125; representative, 72
African American music: in Antebellum period, 5–7; in colorblind culture, 49; informed performance practice of, 117–21; music economy and, 19–22; Patterson on, 48–49; pedagogy, 55–58; in post-World-War II era, 35–40; religion and, 5–6; timeline of, 4, 132; in twenty-first century, 49–50; vocal concert, 24–31
African Americans, education of, 6, 10
African American Vernacular English, 117
African culture, 3; communal music making in, 4–5; music in, 4–5
Afro-American Symphony, 16, 78
Afrocentric Voice in Classical Music, 112
Afrocentrism, 57
"Ah, Love, But a Day!," 73–74
"Ain-a Dat Good News," 86
"All Shook Up," 37
allyship, 108–11; living, 128
Alvin Theater, 16
Amazing Grace, 103, 132
ambivalence, obstacles of, xxv–xxvi
American Bandstand, 45
American culture, whiteness and, 3
American song anthologies: African American, xxvii; African American composers absent from, xxiii
America's Musical Life (Crawford), 35

Anderson, Marian, 16, 23, 24, 25, 87, 87, 130
Antebellum period: African American music in, 5–7; white Americans in, 8–10
An Anthology of African and African Diaspora Songs, 114
Apollo Theater, 16, 102
Appalachian Spring (Copland), 17
Argento, Dominic, 133
Aristotle, 138
Arkansas Youth Symphony, 139
Armstrong, Louis, 70
artists, teaching, 144–45
The Art of the Spiritual (Bibbs), 82
Art Songs by Black American Composers, 45, 77
Arvey, Verna, 40
Atcheson, Sheree, 110
audience, creation of, 145–46

Baker, David, 117–19, 120
Baker, Josephine, 20
The Ballad of Baby Doe, 77
The Ballad of the Brown King, 148
"Balm in Gilead," 86
Barber, Samuel, 78
Barnard College, 76
Barnum, P. T., 6
Basie, Count, 35
A Bayou Legend, 78
Beach, Amy, 73–74
bebop, 35–37
Berry, Chuck, 38
Bethune, Thomas, 6
Bibbs, Cheryl Sushell, 82
Biblical references, in spirituals, 84
Bill Haley and His Comets, 38
Billy the Kid, 16
Black, Brown and Beige, 17
"Black and Blue," 31
Black Arts Movement, 45, 120
The Black Composer Speaks, 128

The Black Experience, 120
Blackface minstrelsy, xviii, xxiv, 22, 39, 128; instrumentation in, 8–9; origins of, 8–9; stereotypes in, 8–9
Black is Beautiful, 49
Black Lives Matter, xviii
Black Music Research Journal, 48
Blackness, 23; stereotype of, 11–12
Black opera, 75–80
The Black Swan, 6
Black Swan Records, 16
Black theology, concert spirituals and, 83–84
Blackwell, Otis, 37
Blake, Eubie, 16, 100
Bland, James, 12
Bloch, Ernst, 76
Bonds, Estella, 43
Bonds, Margaret, 16, 43–44, 131, 133, 148
Bontemps, Arna, 25
The Books of the American Negro Spirituals (Johnson, J. W.), 83
Boston Lyric Opera, 138
Boulanger, Nadia, 76
Boulogne, Joseph, 70
Bowling Green State University, 69
Boyer, Valarino, 144
Brookfield, Stephen D., 126
Brown, Lawrence, 82
Browning, Robert, 73
Brown v. Board of Education, 42
Buchanan, James, 6–7
Burleigh, H. T., xxi, 15, 19, 25–26, 59, 82, 84, 89, 131; Dvořák and, xxiv, 18; "Ride On, King Jesus" arranged by, 87–93; on singing of spirituals, 86
"Bye and Bye," 6

call and response form, 86
Calloway, Cab, 35
Cambridge Dictionary, 108
"Camptown Races," 9

canon, 67; culture and, 68–71
Cantata, xxi
Cantata for baritone, narrator, chorus, and orchestra, 148
Capra, Frank, 91
Carpenter, John Alden, 16
"Carry Me Back to Old Virginny," 12
Carter, John, xxi
Carver, George Washington, 147
"Cassandra's Lullaby," 77
Castle, Irene, 19, 26
Castle, Vernon, 19, 26
Catholic University of America, 69
Cautionary Tales, 68
CBMR. *See* Center for Black Music Research
Census Report, U.S., 140–42
Center for Black Music Research (CBMR), 70
Center for Music Ecosystems, 139
"Cernt'ly Lord (or Have You Got Good Religion?)," 84, 86
Charles Ives Fellowship, 113
Charleston dance, 21
Charlie Pride, 132
chattel slavery, xxviii
Christianity, 83–84; conversion to, 5
A Christmas Miracle, 77
Christy Minstrels, 9
"City Called Heaven," 6, 86
Civil Rights Act of 1964, 42
Civil Rights movement, 40–49; concert music and, 42–44
Clague, Mark, 70
classical music, xxiv, 146–47
Classical Vocal Reprints (CVR), 114
classroom activities, 129–30
classroom teaching, 129–33
Clef Club, 19
Clef Club Orchestra, 15, 19
Cole, Bob, 100
Coleridge-Taylor, Samuel, 19, 70, 131
Collaborative Undergraduate Research & Inquiry Program, 59

College Music Society, 115
colorblind culture, African American music in, 49
The Color Purple, 103
communal music making, 4–5
community arts education, 138–40
community-based music ecosystems, *141*
community-building, 64; for administration and faculty, 125–28
community engagement, 62–64
Community Music Center, 138
"Community Music Education" (Kruse & Hansen), 140
comparative text study, 131
comparison models, 143
concert music: Civil Rights movement and, 42–44; racism and, 38–40
Concerto in F, 21
concerts, attending, 149
concert spirituals, 82–83; Black theology and, 83–84; case studies, 86–100; dialect in, 85; performance of, 84–86; settings for, 86–100
Cone, James, 83
Conference for the International Society of the Scholarship of Teaching and Learning, xxvi
Connie's Hot Chocolates, 31
conservatory training, 6
Cook, Will Marion, 15, 19
Copland, Aaron, 16, 17, 133
correlation or effects position, 142
Cotton Club, 20, 32n12
Cotton Club Orchestra, 16
Crawford, Richard, 31, 36, 37, 38
creative programming, 133–34
Cullen, Countee, 25
cultural competency, 62
cultural humility, 82–83; lifelong education and, 115–16
culturally responsive teaching, 115
cultural responsiveness, 57
culture: canon and, 68–71; shared, 74–75

culture bearers, 144–45
cummings, e. e., 133
Curtis Institute of Music, 78, 101
CVR. *See* Classical Vocal Reprints

Dabri, Emma, 110
D'Angelo, Robin, xxv, 127
Davis, Fanie E., 62
Dawson, William, 16
Debussy, Claude, xxiv
deep listening, 125–27
"Deep River," 85–86, 87; Hogan arrangement of, 97–98; Johnson, J. R., arrangement of, 93–97
Deep River Collection, 98
DEI. *See* diversity, equity, and inclusion
Delibe, Leo, 130
demographics, 140–42
Detroit Civic Orchestra, 16
Detroit Opera, 139
Dett, R. Nathaniel, 31, 82
Devil at the Crossroads, 132
dialect, in concert spirituals, 85
dialogue, *109*
Dickinson, Emily, 133, 134
D'Indy, Vincent, 76
The Discussion Book (Brookfield and Preskill), 126
Disney, Walt, 91
diversity, equity, and inclusion (DEI), 128
"Don't Be Cruel," 37
double consciousness, 71–72
Douglass, Frederick, 147
Dreamgirls, 103
"A Dream Wasted," 78
DuBois, W. E. B., 10, 15, 17, 71, 127; on spirituals, 99
Duke, John, 134
Dunbar, Paul Laurence, xxv, 15, 73, 131, 133
Duncan, Todd, 87

Dvořák, Antonin, 68, 99, 146–47; Burleigh and, xxiv, 18
Dvořák's Prophecy (Horowitz), 23

"Early in the Mornin'," *118*, *119*
Eastman School of Music, 139
economic autonomy, 17–19
education, 17–19, *109*; of African Americans, 6, 10; audience engagement and, 63; lifelong, 115–16. *See also* pedagogy; teachers and teaching
"Elijah Rock," 84, 86
Ellington, Duke, 16, 17, 32n12, 70, 102
Emancipation, 6, 10–12
Emma Louise, 11
empathy, 57
Emperor of Haiti, 40
Encyclopedia of the Harlem Renaissance, 20
equal opportunities, 145–46
essay writing, 131
Eurocentrism, 115
Europe, James Reese, 15, 18–19, 26
Evans, Mari, 120
"Ev'ry Time I Feel the Spirit," 86
expert engagement, case studies, 111–15
"Exploring Racial & Gender Equity Beyond the Concert Hall," 63

faculty: activities for, 128; community-building for, 125–28
Farrell, Eileen, 87
Fax, Mark, 76–77
films, group discussion of, 132
Fisk Jubilee Singers, 11, 23, 81
Fisk University, 10–11
Fitzgerald, Ella, 16, 37, 102
Floyd, George, xviii, 68
Floyd, Samuel, 31, 70
folk songs, 56
Foster, Stephen Collins, 9, 12
Franklin, Aretha, 102, 103, 132

"The French Knight's Guide to Corporate Culture," 68
From Spirituals to Symphonies (Walker-Hill), 43

Garofalo, Reebee, 107–8
George V (King), 23
Gershwin, George, xxiv, 16, 21
"Getting to Know You," 73–74
Giants of the Earth, 76
Gilbert, Henry Franklin Belknap, 99
Gilded Age, 17–18, 77
Gillespie, Dizzy, 36
"Give Me Jesus," 85–86
"Go Down Moses," 86
Goodman, Bennie, 35
Google Slides, 132–33
Gordy, Berry, 41
gospel music, xxiv–xxv, 99; case studies, 101–3; spirituals distinguished from, 85
Grammy awards, 69
Grant, Ulysses S., 11
the Grateful Dead, 41
"Great Balls of Fire," 37
Great Depression, 39, 76
Great Migration, 20
Greenfield, E. H., 6
Greenfield, Elizabeth Taylor, 6
Grinnell College, 112–13
group discussions, 127
group text study, 130
guest speakers, 144–45

Hailstork, Adolphus, 50, 131
Hair, 45
Haiti, 40
Haley, Alex, 45
half consciousness, 71
Hall Johnson Negro Choir, 16, 26
The Hall Johnson Spirituals (Simpson), 91
Hall Johnson Spirituals prize, 99
Hamilton, 103

Hamm, Charles, 8, 38
Hammerstein, Oscar, II, 16
Handel, George Fridrich, 138–39
Handy, W. C., 15, 18–19
Hansen, Eric, 140
Hanson, Howard, 76, 78
Harford, Tim, 68
Harlem Renaissance, xix, 31, 38–39, 59, 74, 134; music in, 23–25; origination of, 20. *See also* New Negro movement
Hatch, James, 44
Haydn, Joseph, 138–39
Hayes, Roland, 23, 24, 25, 84, 87
HBCUs. *See* historically Black colleges and universities
Helms, 143–44
Helton, Caroline, xxi–xxii
Hendrix, Jimi, 41, 149
"He Never Said a Mumblin' Word," 5
Henry Louis Gates, 132
"He's got the Whole World in His Hands," 5
Highway 1, 78–79
Hill, Abram, 17
hip hop, 121n12
historically Black colleges and universities (HBCUs), 24–25, 26
Hitsville, 132
Hogan, Moses, 97; "Deep River" arranged by, 97–98
Hogges, Genithia, 24–25
Holiday, Billie, 40–41
Horowitz, Joseph, 23, 127
"Hound Dog," 37
House Un-American Activities Committee, 39, 40
Howard, Theresa Ruth, 144
Howard University, 76–77
"How We Speak" (Evans), 120
Hughes, Langston, xvii, 25, 44, 74, 133, 148; dialect used by, 26–27; leftist activism of, 40
humility, cultural. *See* cultural humility

Hurston, Zora Neale, 81
Hyers Sisters, 11
hypotheses, writing, 142–43

I am a Black Woman (Evans), 120
ignorance, obstacles of, xxiii–xxiv
"I Got a Robe," 84, 86
inclusivity, 58
independent statements, 142
"Industrializing African American Popular Music" (Garofalo), 107–8
I Never Walked Naked Alone, 42
influence, 74–75
informed performance practice, 117–21
informed research, 59–62
In Square Circle, 102
institutionalized racism, xxviii
interracial collaborations, 19–22
"In the Springtime," 74
Into the Woods, 102

the Jackson 5, 41
jazz: case studies, 101–3; in post-World War II era, 35–37
Jim Crow, 20, 38, 49; barriers from, 22–24
Johnson, Hall, 16, 25–26, 82, 84, 90; "Ride On, King Jesus" arranged by, 87–93
Johnson, James P., xxiv, 21–22
Johnson, James Weldon, 15, 20, 83
Johnson, J. Rosamond, 31
Johnson, Rosamond, 19, 82; "Deep River" arranged by, 93–97
Jones, Glendower, 114–15
Jones, Quincy, 81
Jones, Randye, 111, 112–13
Jones, Sissieretta, 11
Joplin, Janis, 41
Joplin, Scott, 15, 23
"Joshua Fit de Battle O' Jericho," 84
Juilliard School, 113
Julius Rosenwald Fellowship, 76
"Jump Jim Crow," 8

Kern, Jerome, 16
Kernodle, Tammy, 40
King, Betty Jackson, 74
King, Martin Luther, Jr., 50
Kinnard, J., 9
Klotman, Robert, 117
Knickerbocker Magazine, 9
Kpelle people, 4
Kruse, Nathan, 140

Ladson-Billings, Gloria, 115
Lakme, 130
Lamont, Amélie, 108
Lang, James, 56
learning inventories, 129–30
learning outcomes, 129
Lewis, Jerry Lee, 37
lifelong education, cultural humility and, 115–16
Lind, Jenny, 6
listening, deep, 125–27
"Litany," 74
A Little Devil in America (D'Angelo), 127
Little Richard, 38
Locke, Alain, 146–47
Lost Horizon, 91
Lotus Chamber Music Collective, 63
lynching, 38
Lyre Club Symphony, 130

Madah, Anna, 11
Manhattan School of Community Partnerships Program, 139
Ma Rainey's Black Bottom, 132
Marian Anderson (documentary), 132
Marshall, Arthur, 15
Martha and the Vandellas, 41
Maultsby, Portia, 4
Maynor, Dorothy, 25
McCormack, John, 87
McFerrin, Robert, 39
McKnight Composers Fellowship, 113
Meeropol, Abel, 40–41

Menotto, Gian Carlo, 77–78
Merritt, Myra, 69
Met Competition, 46, 48
Metropolitan Opera, 69
Metropolitan Opera Auditions of the Air, 39, 50n9
Metropolitan Opera National Council Award, 48
Michigan Opera, 139
Michigan Philharmonic, 139
Michigan School of Music, Theatre & Dance, xxi
Miles Davis, 132
Milhaud, Darius, xxiv, 68
Miller, Glenn, 35
mindfulness, 57
Miranda, Lin-Manuel, 103
Monk, Thelonius, 36
Moore, Douglas, 76, 77
Moses Hogan Singers, 98
"Mother to Son" (Hughes), 26–27, 27, 28, 29, 30
Motown Record Corporation, 41
Moya, Reinaldo, 111, 113–14
multidisciplinary practices, 57
music, defining, 137–38
musical theatre, popular music and, 100–103
Music Appreciation class, xxvii
music economy, African American music and, 19–22
music ecosystems, 123–24; community-based, *141*; institutional model, *124*
Music Educators National Conference, 117
Music History class, xxvii
The Music of Black Americans (Southern), 7, 8–9
Musto, John, 74

National Association for the Advancement of Colored People (NAACP), 15; establishment of, 20
National Association of Negro Musicians (NANM), 16, 43, 45
National Association of Teachers of Singing (NATS), 100, 112, 135n5, 144
National Geographic Magazine, 42
National Guild for Community Arts Education, 138–40
Native American culture, 3
NATS. *See* National Association of Teachers of Singing
Nazism, 35
Negro Folk Symphony, 16
"The Negro Speaks of Rivers" (Bonds, M.), 44
"Nelly Bly," 9
"Nelly was a lady," 9
neo-spirituals, 81–82
networking, 146–48
New England Conservatory, 10
New Negro movement, values of, 24–25
New World Symphony, xxiv, 68
noble savage, 6–7
"Nobody Knows the Trouble I've Seen," 86
non-classical genres, spirituals and, 98–99
Northam, Ralph, xxvi
Northwestern University, 43–44

Obama, Barack, xix
Oberlin College, 10, 139
"Oh, Dem Golden Slippers," 12
"Oh, Susanna," 9
"Oh Freedom," 41
"Old Folks at Home," 9, 12
The Old Maid and the Thief, 77–80
Old Testament, 5
"Old Uncle Ned," 9
Oluo, 143
O'Neal, Frederick, 17
Ono, Sasha, 63
opera: Black, 75–80; Still composing, 38, 39–40

oral traditions, 3
"Overjoyed," 102–3
"Over My Head," 86

Pace, Harry, 16, 19
Pace & Handy Music Company, 15, 18
Pasek, Benj, 102
paternalism, 110
Patterson, Willis, xxii, 45, 77; on African American music, 48–49
Paul, Justin, 102
Paul Whiteman and His Concert Orchestra, 16
Peabody Conservatory of Music, 69
pedagogy, 55–58
performance, 58–59, 109, 137; of concert spirituals, 84–86; informed performance practice, 117–21; preparation, 140–43; race-specific performance projects, 143–44
permission, 116–17
Perry, Julia, 148
"Peter go ring-a dem bells," xxi
Pick, Margaret Moos, 21
Piper, Scott, 114
Plant, Lourin, 63
playlists, annotated, 132–33
podcasts, 133
Poole, Valter, 16
popular music, 37–38; case studies, 101–3; defining, 100–101; musical theatre and, 100–103
Porgy and Bess, xxiv, 16, 22
PowerPoint, 132–33
Praise of Black Performance (Abdurraquib), 127
"Prayer (2)," 74
Preskill, Stephen, 126
Presley, Elvis, 37
Price, Florence, 16, 31, 70, 73–74, 131
Prohibition, 20
Project for Public Spaces, 145–46
publishing houses, xxiii
Purlie, 45

Questlove, 42, 43

A Race Is A Nice Thing to Have (Helms), 143–44
race music, 19, 38
race-specific performance projects, 143–44
racism, xviii, xxv; concert music and, 38–40; institutionalized, xxviii
Raisin in the Sun, 132
Ravel, Maurice, xxiv, 68
Razaf, Andy, 31
Reckling, Frances Kraft, 43–44
Reconstruction, 10–12
Recorded Solo Concert Spirituals, 1916-2022, 112
reflective practices, 57
Reinert Center for Transformative Teaching and Learning, 56
relationship-building, 146–48
religion, African American music and, 5–6
reparations, 148
Requiem for the Enslaved, 148
research projects, 132–33; preparation, 140–43
responsibility. *See* shared responsibility
restorative justice, 63–64
"Return to Sender," 37
Rhapsody in Blue, 16, 21
rhythm and blues, 37–38; case studies, 101–3
Rice, Thomas Dartmouth, 8
"Ride On, King Jesus," 86; Burleigh arrangement of, 87–93; Johnson, H., arrangement of, 87–93
Roach, Hal, 91
Robeson, Paul, xxviii, 20, 25, 39, 87
Robinson, Smokey, 41
rock and roll, 37–38
Rome, David, 125
Roosevelt, Eleanor, 24
Roots, 45

Ross, Diana, 41
Rowman & Littlefield Publishers, 112
Run, Little Chillun', 16, 91

Saint Louis University, 56
Saint-Saens, 19
Samson and Delilah, 19
scat singing, 36
Scholarship of Multicultural Teaching and Learning, xxvi
Schwartz, Stephen, 102
"Sea Ghost," 43
segregation, 10; barriers from, 22–24
Shadow of the Blues, 74
Shakespeare, William, 74
Shapiro, Shain, 139
shared culture, 74–75
shared responsibility, 116–17
Shostakovich, xxiv
shout-style spirituals, 86
Shuffle Along, 23, 26, 100
Simon, Carlos, 148
Simon Bolivar Orchestra, 113
Simone, Nina, 41, 45, 101
Simpson, Eugene Thamon, 91
"Singing African-American Spirituals," 63
Singing Down the Barriers, 69, 139; 1.0, xxvi–xxvii
Sissle, Noble, 16, 100
Six, 103
slavery, 9, 128
slave songs, 11
Small Teaching (Lang), 56
Smith-Moore, Undine, 128, 131
Snow White and the Seven Dwarfs, 91
"Sometimes I Feel Like a Motherless Child," 86
song case studies, 73–75
Songs of Love and Justice, 50
Son of Man, 148
"Sopranos Without Borders," 133
sorrow songs, 85–86
soul music, 134; case studies, 101–3

The Souls of Black Folks (DuBois), 15, 127
Soul Train, 45
South African Truth and Reconciliation Commission, 14n28
Southeastern Minnesota Art Council, 145
Southern, Eileen, 7, 8–9, 23
So You Want to Talk About Race (Oluo), 143
Spanish Civil War, 40
spirituals, 56; Biblical references in, 84; Burleigh on singing of, 86; call and response form, 86; classification of, 84–85; concert performance of, xxi–xxii; DuBois on, 99; gospel music distinguished from, 85; non-classical genres and, 98–99; origins of, 5–6; pedagogy of, xxi–xxii; shout-style, 86; sorrow songs, 85–86; traveling, 86. *See also* concert spiritual
The Spirituals Database, 112
The Spirituals of Harry T. Burleigh, 87
"Star Spangled Banner," 41
Star Tribune, 113
"Steal Away to Jesus," 85–86
Stephens, Emery, xxi–xxii, xxvii, 60
stereotypes: barriers from, 22–24; in Blackface minstrelsy, 8–9; of Blackness, 11–12
Still, William Grant, xxiv, 16, 19, 26, 31, 70, 78–80, 131; opera compositions, 39–40
"St. Louis Blues," 15
Stokowski, Leopold, 16, 40, 42
St. Olaf College, 59
Stowe, Harriet Beecher, 6, 9–10
"Strange Fruit," 40–41
students: approaches to learning for, 129–33; teachers and, 61
Summer of Soul, 42, 132
Sunday In The Park With George, 102
the Supremes, 41
Swanson, Howard, 130

Sweeney Todd, 102
swing, 35–37
"Swing Low, Sweet Chariot," 6, 86
"Sympathy," 73–74
Syracuse University, 76

Talissé, Chesley, 137
Tatum, 144
teachers and teaching, 67; artists, 144–45; in classroom, 129–33; culturally responsive, 115; students and, 61
text studies, 130–31
Thomas, Henry V. S., 129
Thornton, Big Mama, 37
Three Browning Songs, 73
Three Dream Portraits (Bonds, M.), 44
Thurber, Jeannette Meyers, 17–18
Thurman, Kira, 125
Tienda, 113
Till, Emmett, 38
Tin Pan Alley, 19–20, 22, 37
Toppin, Louise, 70, 114, 135n5
Toscanini, Arturo, 23–24
"Transforming Music Study from its Foundations," 115
"The Translated African Cultural and Musical Past" (Maultsby), 4
trauma, 57
traveling spirituals, 86
A Trip to Coontown, 100
Troubled Island, 39, 40, 78
Tulsa, 148
Turtle Creek Chorale, 148

Uncle Tom's Cabin (Stowe), 9–10
University of Michigan, xxii, 135n5; School of Music, Theatre & Dance, 70

Van Lier Fellowship, 113
Van Vechten, Carl, 20
Vaughan, Sarah, 36, 37
Verrett, Shirley, 42–43

vocal concert music, 24–31
vocal training, 98–99

Wade, Ray M., Jr., 45, 47, 48
"Wade in de Water," 6, 86
Walker, George, 70
Walker, Madam C. J., 147
Walker-Hill, Helen, 43
Waller, Fats, 21
Wanamaker Competition for Negro Composers, 16
Washington, Booker T., 10, 17, 104n24
Waters, Ethel, 19, 20
"We, Too, Sing America," 131
West Virginia University, 113
What Do You Know About Blacks in Classical Music (Thomas), 59, 129–30
White, George L., 10–11
White, Paul, 16
white composers, representative, 72
White Fragility (DiAngelo), xxv, 143
whiteness: American culture and, 3; societal lens of, xxv
Whitman, Walt, 133
Why Are All the Black Kids Sitting Together in the Cafeteria? (Tatum), 144
Williams, Martin, 36–37
"The Willow Song," 77
Wilson, Flip, 45
"Witness," 86
Wonder, Stevie, 41, 102
Woodstock, 41
Work, John Wesley, 82
World War I, 59
World War II, 35

Yamekraw, A Negro Rhapsody, 21
"Young, Gifted and Black," 45
YouTube, 133

Zenobia, 91

About the Authors

Emery Stephens, a native of Boston, is co-founder of the "Singing Down the Barriers Project," which engages interdisciplinary dialogue through the diverse representation and performance of works by Black composers in the canon. He has delivered presentations for the College Music Society, Race and Pedagogy National Conference, African American Art Song Alliance, National Association for the Study and Performance of African American Music, and the Singing Down the Barriers Institute. He is also an active singer and enjoys teaching and inspiring students on the music faculty at St. Olaf College.

Caroline Helton is a pedagogue, performer, and researcher who teaches voice in the Department of Musical Theatre at the University of Michigan School of Music, Theatre & Dance. As a performer, she has recorded classic song repertoire by composers whose art was suppressed, and through her teaching, recordings, and publications, she is a tireless advocate for integrating the canon of song repertoire to reflect and respect its true diversity. She has been collaborating with Dr. Emery Stephens since 2004 on the "Singing Down the Barriers Project."

www.ingramcontent.com/pod-product-compliance
Lightning Source LLC
Chambersburg PA
CBHW032045300426
44117CB00009B/1200